Student Applications Book

Great Source Education Group

a Houghton Mifflin Company

Wilmington, Massachusetts

www.greatsource.com

AUTHORS

Jim Burke
Author

Burlingame High School, Burlingame, California
Jim Burke, author of *Reading Reminders: Tools, Tips, and Techniques* and *The English Teacher's Companion*, has taught high school English for 13 years. His most recent books, *Tools for Thought* and *Illuminating Texts: How to Teach Students to Read the World*, further explore reading and those strategies that can help all students succeed in high school. He was the recipient of the California Reading Association's Hall of Fame Award in 2001 and the Conference on English Leadership's Exemplary English Leadership Award in 2000. He currently serves on the National Board of Professional Teaching Standards for English Language Arts.

Ron Klemp
Contributing Author

Los Angeles Unified School District, Los Angeles, California
Ron Klemp is the Coordinator of Reading for the Los Angeles Unified School District. He has taught Reading, English, and Social Studies and was a middle school Dean of Discipline. He is also a coordinator/facilitator at the Secondary Practitioner Center, a professional development program in the Los Angeles Unified School District. He has been teaching at California State University, Cal Lutheran University, and National University.

Wendell Schwartz
Contributing Author

Adlai Stevenson High School, Lincolnshire, Illinois
Wendell Schwartz has been a teacher of English for 36 years. For the last 24 years he also has served as the Director of Communication Arts at Adlai Stevenson High School. He has taught gifted middle school students for the last 12 years, as well as teaching graduate-level courses for National Louis University in Evanston, Illinois.

Editorial:
Design:
Illustrations:

Developed by Nieman, Inc. with Phil LaLeike
Ronan Design: Christine Ronan, Sean O'Neill, Maria Mariottini, Victoria Mullins
Mike McConnell

Printed in the United States of America

International Standard Book Number: 0-669-49507-7
(Student Applications Book)

1 2 3 4 5 6 7 8 9—DBH—09 08 07 06 05 04 03 02

International Standard Book Number: 0-669-49512-3
(Student Applications Book, Teacher's Edition)

1 2 3 4 5 6 7 8 9—DBH—09 08 07 06 05 04 03 02

Table of Contents for Student Applications Book

Lessons

What Is Reading?

Have you heard the saying "every reader reads alone"? It means that you and you alone control your understanding of a text.

What reading is to me

You can train to become a good reader in the same way that an athlete trains. Begin by asking yourself, "What does reading mean to me?"

Directions: Reread pages 26–27 in the *Reader's Handbook*. Then, write your reactions to the following sentences.

Understanding Reading

Reading is working:

Reading is thinking:

Reading is imagining:

NAME

B Preview

Always preview a textbook chapter before reading. Look at the title, the study guide or goals box, the first and last paragraphs, and any background information. Also pay attention to repeated or boldface words.

Directions: Preview "The Supreme Court." Write your notes on the stickies.

Preview Notes

What is the title of the chapter? What is it mostly about? *The Supreme Court government*

What did you notice in the study guide box?

What did you learn from the first and last paragraphs? *Supreme court is often called "court of court"*

What repeated and boldface terms did you notice? *to do with court*

Chapter 5
The Supreme Court

Key Terms and Concepts

• checks and balances
• judicial review
• appeal
• confirmed
• the rule of four
• brief
• majority opinion
• concurring opinion
• dissenting opinion

Goals

As you read, look for answers to these questions:

1. Why is the Supreme Court often referred to as the "court of last resort"?
2. What are some of the duties of a Supreme Court justice?
3. What does it mean when the Court publishes its "opinion"?

The Supreme Court is the highest court in the United States judicial system. It is the final authority on all cases involving the Constitution, Acts of Congress, and treaties with other nations. For this reason, the Supreme Court is often called the "court of last resort."

The Supreme Court is a key feature of the American system of government. It is the "umpire" in any disagreement between state and nation, state and state, and government and citizen. There is no higher authority in the land.

Stop and Think: What and Why

What is the Supreme Court? Why is it important? Make some reporter's notes on page 26.

Purpose of the Court

The Supreme Court is the only court that is directly mentioned in the United States Constitution. The Framers of the Constitution did this for an important reason. Their goal was to establish a court that would be on equal footing with the president and Congress. In effect, they gave the Supreme Court the right to oversee the work of the other two branches of government. The president and Congress, in turn, were given the right to oversee the work of the Supreme Court.

This three-armed balance of power is an example of checks and balances. **Checks and balances** is a system by which political power is divided among the three branches of government, with each having some control over the others.

The Court's power to oversee the actions of the legislative, executive, and administrative arms of the government is called the power of **judicial review**. Much of the time, the Court uses this power to hear cases in which the constitutionality of a law or action is being questioned. These cases come to the Court in the form of an **appeal,** or request for a new trial.

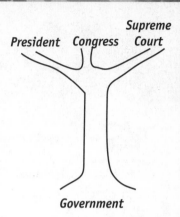

President   Congress   Supreme Court

Government

The Court at Work

For the first eighty or so years after the Constitution was ratified, the number of justices serving on the Court fluctuated between eight and ten. This fluctuation caused a great deal of arguing between political parties. To solve the problem, Congress fixed the number of justices at nine in 1869. This number cannot be changed without the approval of the Senate and the House of Representatives.

Today, the Supreme Court is made up of the Chief Justice of the United States and eight associate justices. All nine of the justices serve for life, although Congress has the right to impeach a justice for bad behavior.

Only the president can appoint a justice to the Supreme Court. Before the justice can take a seat on the Court, however, he or she must be **confirmed,** or ratified, by Congress.

The building in which the Supreme Court resides is nicknamed "The Marble Palace."

Stop and Think: How

How does someone become a Supreme Court judge? Make some notes on page 26.

Supreme Court Justices, 2002

Justice	Appointing President	Year Appointed
William H. Rehnquist (Chief Justice of the United States)	Richard Nixon	1971
John Paul Stevens	Gerald Ford	1975
Sandra Day O'Connor	Ronald Reagan	1981
Antonin Scalia	Ronald Reagan	1986
Anthony M. Kennedy	Ronald Reagan	1988
David H. Souter	George Bush	1990
Clarence Thomas	George Bush	1991
Ruth Bader Ginsburg	Bill Clinton	1993
Stephen G. Breyer	Bill Clinton	1994

Focus Question *Which justice on today's Court has served the longest? Which justice was appointed most recently to the Court?*

Stop and Think: Who

Who are today's Supreme Court justices? Make some reporter's notes on page 26.

Supreme Court Duties

The main duty of a Supreme Court justice is to hear and rule on cases. To fulfill this duty, the Court completes a series of four important steps:

1. Decide which cases will be heard.
2. Hear the oral arguments.
3. Rule on the case.
4. Publish the opinion.

Choosing the Cases. As a first step, the justices must choose the cases they want to hear. Of the thousands of cases submitted to the Supreme Court in a given year, only a few hundred are accepted for review. No case is accepted unless four of the nine justices have agreed that the case should be put on the Court's docket. This is called **"the rule of four."**

24

Hearing the Arguments. Next, the justices hear the cases. The hearings for Supreme Court cases are public. The Court is in session on Mondays, Tuesdays, Wednesdays, and sometimes Thursdays. Lawyers for both sides of an issue are given a specified amount of time to make their case. To help the justices sort through the complex issues, they are given briefs by the lawyers arguing the cases. A **brief** presents legal arguments, historical materials, and related previous decisions.

Ruling on the Case. As a third step, the justices rule on the cases. They do this by holding private case conferences a couple of times a week. The chief justice presides over each conference and speaks first, usually indicating how he or she intends to vote. Next, the eight associate justices are given the chance to air their own opinions. Lively debates often follow the "polling" of the justices. The debates end with an official vote on the case. In some cases, all nine judges will vote the same way. Other times, the justices split on an issue. When this happens, majority rules.

Publishing the Opinion. As a final step, the justices publish the Court's opinion, which is an announcement and explanation of the Court's decision. If the chief justice has voted with the majority, he or she writes the opinion. If the chief justice has voted with the minority, a senior justice on the majority side will write the opinion. The official opinion of the Court is called the **majority opinion.** Sometimes, another justice or two will write a **concurring opinion** to explain why they agree with the majority opinion. Justices in the minority may publish a **dissenting opinion.** Here, the justice explains why he or she *disagrees* with the majority decision.

Stop and Think: When and Where

When and where does the Supreme Court meet? Make some reporter's notes on page 26.

C Plan

After your preview, make a reading plan. How can you best meet your purpose? The strategy of note-taking can help.

• **Note-taking can help you process and remember what you've learned.**

During Reading

D Read with a Purpose

Keep your purpose in mind as you read. Remember that you are looking for answers to *who, what, where, when, why,* and *how.*

Directions: Now do a careful reading of the chapter. Make reporter's notes as you go. Record them below. Highlight any important terms or phrases.

Reporter's Notes

The Supreme Court

Who

Where

Why is it important?

What

When

How does someone become a Supreme Court Judge?

Using the Strategy

Now use your strategy of note-taking to help you achieve your purpose. It's important that you choose the tool that works best for you. Many students find that Key Word or Topic Notes (see page 81 of the *Reader's Handbook*) help them get more from a history chapter. Often, but not always, the key words you use will be the boldface terms.

Directions: Write Key Word or Topic Notes for the Supreme Court chapter.

Key Word or Topic Notes

Key Words	Notes
"court of last resort"	
Framers of the Constitution	
three-armed balance of power	
judicial review	
appeal	
"the rule of four"	
majority opinion	
concurring opinion	
dissenting opinion	

Understanding How History Chapters Are Organized

Most history chapters or articles open with a study guide or goals box. Be sure you understand every term and can answer every question in this box.

• **Use the study guide or goals box to help you figure out what's most important in the chapter.**

Directions: Return to the goals box on page 22. Answer the questions and define the key terms.

1. Why is the Supreme Court often referred to as the "court of last resort"?

....

....

2. What are some of the duties of a Supreme Court justice?

....

....

3. What does it mean when the Court publishes its opinion?

....

....

• checks and balances—

....

....

• judicial review—

....

• appeal—

....

• confirmed—

....

• rule of four—

....

....

• brief—

....

....

• majority opinion—

....

• concurring opinion—

....

....

• dissenting opinion—

....

....

NAME

 E **Connect**

Connecting to a history text means getting involved in a personal way with the reading.

• **Imagining yourself a part of history can help you make a strong connection to what you've read.**

Directions: Imagine yourself a Supreme Court justice. Which of the four duties discussed on pages 24–25 would you find the most difficult? Why?

The duty that would be most difficult for me would be

....

....

....

After Reading

When you finish reading, take a moment or two to think about what you did and did not understand about the chapter.

 F **Pause and Reflect**

Reflect on your original reading purpose.

• **Ask yourself three important questions about your purpose and what you've learned.**

Directions: Answer these three questions about the reading.

1. Did I meet the reading purpose I set in the beginning?
....

2. Do I know answers to the five W's?
....

3. Do I know enough details to be able to discuss the ideas in the chapter

intelligently?
....

 G **Reread**

Now return to the text. Reread and look for details you missed the first time around.

• **Use graphic organizers to help you get more from your second reading.**

Textbooks

29

Directions: Use a web organizer to help you group important facts and details from the Supreme Court chapter.

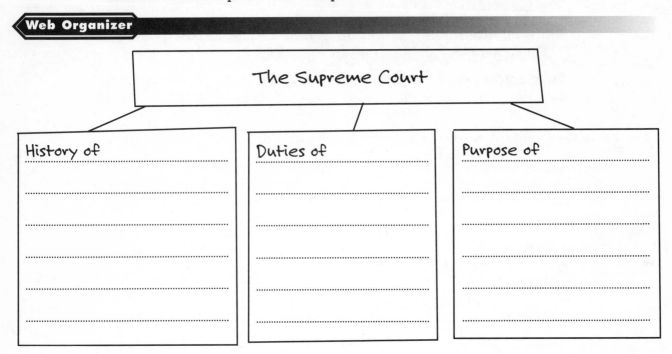

The Supreme Court

| History of | Duties of | Purpose of |

Remember

Good readers remember what they've read.

• **Conducting an "interview" about the subject can help you remember what you've read.**

Directions: Write three interview questions on the lines below. Then, exchange books and have a partner answer them.

Question 1

Answer:

Question 2

Answer:

Question 3

Answer:

NAME ....

FOR USE WITH PAGES 88–99

Reading Science

If you're having trouble understanding science, it may be because of how you're reading the textbook. Good readers know strategies that can help them get more from every chapter.

Before Reading

Use the reading process and the strategy of outlining to help you read and understand a science textbook chapter about igneous rocks.

A   Set a Purpose

Your purpose when reading a science chapter is to find out as much as you can about the subject.

> • **To set your purpose, turn the title of the chapter into a question.**

__Directions:__ Write your purpose for reading "Igneous Rocks" on the lines below. Then, write what you expect to learn from the chapter.

My purpose: ....

....

....

Here are three things I expect to learn from this chapter: ....

1. ....

....

2. ....

....

3. ....

....

Textbooks

B Preview

Preview a science chapter first, so that you know what to expect during your careful reading. Pay particular attention to the items on this checklist:

Preview Checklist

- ☐ title
- ☐ the first and last paragraphs
- ☐ headings
- ☐ boxed items
- ☐ words in boldface or repeated words
- ☐ any photos, charts, or pictures

Directions: Skim the science chapter that begins on page 33. Place a check mark beside each feature as you preview it. Then make notes on the Preview Chart below.

Preview Chart

The titles and headings tell me . . .	I noticed these boldface words . . .

Igneous Rocks

The art tells me . . .	I expect to learn . . .

NAME ....

Chapter 11.2 | Igneous Rocks

Study Guide • • • • • • • • • • • • • • • • • • •

Objectives
• Learn the origins, features, and types of igneous rocks.
• Differentiate between extrusive and intrusive igneous rocks.

Terms to Know

igneous rocks	crystals
magma	extrusive igneous rocks
lava	intrusive igneous rocks

Did you know that an airplane is made of rocks? It's true! But the rocks you're thinking of are not the rocks an aviation designer uses to build a plane. Instead, the designer uses the iron and other metals that are extracted from several different types of rocks. The most important of these are called igneous rocks.

Igneous rocks are crystalline or glassy rocks that are formed by the cooling and solidification of magma. Igneous rocks, along with sedimentary and metamorphic rocks, make up three principal classes of rocks.

| Igneous | Sedimentary | Metamorphic |

There are three main classes. Most rock is made up of two or more minerals.

The Origin of Igneous Rock

Igneous rocks form when hot melted material, called **magma,** cools and becomes solid rock. Usually this process occurs well beneath the surface of the Earth.

Sometimes, however, magma breaks the surface of the Earth at a volcano and cools above ground. When this happens, the magma is called **lava.** When lava cools, it too forms igneous rock.

Stop and Organize
Make notes in the first section of your outline on page 36.

The Role of Crystals

Crystals, which are solids with atoms arranged in a regular, repeating pattern, are the building blocks of rock. When magma or lava cools from a liquid to a solid, crystals form.

Sometimes the cooling rock material yields crystals large enough to be made into jewelry. Other times, the rock crystals are so tiny that they are invisible to the naked eye.

The length of cooling time determines the size of the rock crystals. Rock material that cools slowly forms larger crystals. Rock material that cools quickly forms smaller crystals.

Stop and Organize

Make notes in the second section of your outline on page 36.

Two Types of Igneous Rocks

The rate of cooling from liquid to solid helps scientists divide igneous rocks into two categories: extrusive and intrusive. **Extrusive igneous rocks** are formed when lava cools on the surface of the Earth. Since lava cools quickly, there is little time for crystals to form. For this reason extrusive igneous rocks have relatively small crystals.

The small crystal size of extrusive igneous rocks makes these rocks less valuable to humans. Although they can be crushed and processed as gravel for highways, most extrusive igneous rocks are mainly interesting additions to the landscape.

The counterparts to extrusive igneous rocks

The Obsidian Cliffs in Yellowstone National Park are made of a type of glassy extrusive igneous rock called obsidian.

"Igneous Rocks"

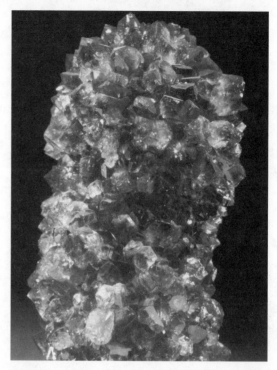

are **intrusive igneous rocks.** Intrusive igneous rocks are formed when magma cools beneath the earth's surface. Many types of valuable metals such as iron, copper, and gold can be found in intrusive igneous rocks.

Like all igneous rocks, intrusive igneous rocks start out as magma. But the magma that solidifies into this type of rock begins cooling *before* it reaches the Earth's surface. The rate of cooling underground is slower than on the surface because other rocks act as blankets for the cooling rocks. This allows more time for crystal growth. As a result, the crystals in intrusive igneous rocks can be quite large. In many cases, the minerals found within these crystals are highly sought after.

Exotic minerals present in igneous rocks include amethysts, garnets, and zircons.

Stop and Organize

Make notes in the third section of your outline on page 36.

C Plan

Now that you've previewed the science chapter, make a plan. Choose a strategy that can help you meet your reading purpose.

• An excellent strategy to use with science chapters is outlining.

Before you begin reading, create an Outline using the grid on page 36. Use the major headings in the chapter as the major headings in your Outline.

Textbooks

During Reading

D Read with a Purpose

Make notes on stickies as you read. Add the most important facts and details to your outline.

Directions: Now do a careful reading of the science chapter. Write your notes on this Outline.

Outline

I. The origin of igneous rocks

A.

B.

II. The role of crystals

A.

B.

C.

III. Two types of igneous rocks

A.

   1.

   2.

B.

   1.

   2.

     a.

     b.

NAME ....

Understanding How Science Texts Are Organized

Scientists often think in terms of cause and effect. Many science chapters are organized around this concept.

Directions: Reread the information about magma in the science chapter. Then complete the following organizer.

Cause-Effect Organizer

Effects

Cause

Hot magma formed under the Earth's surface begins rising above ground.

E Connect

As often as possible, make personal connections to a science chapter. These connections can help you remember what you've read.

• **You can connect to a science chapter by noting what the subject reminds you of from your own life.**

Directions: Reread this paragraph from the science chapter. Then, make some connection notes on the sticky.

The small crystal size of extrusive igneous rocks makes these rocks less valuable to humans. Although they can be crushed and processed as gravel for highways, most extrusive igneous rocks are mainly interesting additions to the landscape.

After Reading

When you finish a chapter, try to recall what you have learned. Use your outline to help you review.

F Pause and Reflect

Before moving on, stop and decide whether you've understood everything discussed in the science chapter.

• **Always return to your original reading purpose and see if you've accomplished what you set out to do.**

Directions: Answer these questions about the science chapter you just read.

Looking Back

Did I accomplish the reading purpose I set in the beginning?

Do I know what the main topics in the chapter are?

In my Outline, can I support each main topic with subtopics?

Would I feel comfortable taking a test on this material now?

 Reread

It's unlikely that you'll be able to absorb every fact and detail with just one reading. Plan on rereading at least part of every chapter.

• **A powerful rereading strategy to use is note-taking.**

Directions: Make notes about key terms from the chapter on these study cards.

Study Cards

> 1. magma
> 2. lava

> 1. intrusive igneous rocks
> 2. extrusive igneous rocks

NAME ....

 Remember

Good readers remember what they've read. Creating a practice test can help.

• **Testing yourself will help you remember the most important parts of a science chapter.**

Directions: Write sample test questions. Then, exchange books with a partner and have your partner answer them.

◁ **Practice Test**

Name of Partner

1. Question:

Answer:

2. Question:

Answer:

3. Question:

Answer:

4. Question:

Answer:

Textbooks

Reading Math

To succeed in math, you must know how to read carefully, think critically, and apply what you've learned. Practice using the reading process with a math chapter here.

Before Reading

In math, one concept builds on another like rungs on a ladder. If you skip a rung, you're heading for trouble.

A Set a Purpose

In most cases, you can set your purpose by turning the title of the chapter into questions.

> • **To set your purpose, ask one or more questions about the title of the chapter.**

Directions: On the lines below, write your purpose for reading a math chapter called "Solving Addition Equations."

Purpose question #1

....

....

Purpose question #2

....

....

B Preview

It's vitally important that you preview a math chapter. This will help you recall what you already know about the subject.

Directions: Preview the math chapter that follows. Make notes on the preview chart on the next page. You will fill in the third column later.

Preview Chart

What I Already Know	What I Need to Learn	What I Learned

Textbooks

Chapter
6.1 Solving Addition Equations

Goals
- Learn how to solve addition equations.
- Understand how to use addition equations to solve real-life problems.

Key Terms
addition equation
variable

Goal 1 Solving addition equations

An addition equation is a mathematical statement that is solved through the use of addition. To solve an addition equation, subtract the same number from both sides of the equation so that the variable will be by itself on one side of the equation.

Example 1 Solve this addition equation.

$x + 7 = -4$

Solution

$\begin{aligned} x + 7 &= -4 \quad \text{Original equation} \\ -7 &\quad -7 \quad \text{First, subtract 7 from both sides of the equation} \\ x &= -11 \quad \text{Solution} \end{aligned}$

The solution is −11. You can check your answer this way:

Check:

$\begin{aligned} x + 7 &= -4 \quad \text{Original equation} \\ -11 + 7 &= -4 \quad \text{Substitute −11 for } x \\ -4 &= -4 \quad \text{Both sides are the same} \end{aligned}$

✔ Study Tip
Use mental math to solve addition equations when you can. But be sure you also know how to solve them step-by-step on paper.

Example 2 Solve the addition equation.

$$4 = n + 8$$

Solution

$4 = n + 8$		Original equation
-8	-8	Subtract 8 from both sides of the equation
$-4 = n$		Solution

The solution is -4. Check your solution by returning to the original equation.

Goal 2 Solving Addition Equations in Real Life

Knowing how to solve addition equations can help you solve real-life problems that involve increases and decreases. For example, you use an addition equation if you want to find out how much the outdoor temperature has changed from one day to the next.

Example 3 On a Tuesday in March, the high temperature for the day was 3°. By Friday, the temperature rose to 27°. How many degrees did the temperature climb from Tuesday to Friday?

Solution

The way to solve this problem is to create an addition equation. Let t represent the unknown temperature.

$t + 3° = 27°$	Original equation
$-3°$ $-3°$	First, subtract $-3°$ from both sides of the equation.
$t = 24°$	Solution

The solution is 24°. This means that the temperature climbed 24° between Tuesday and Friday.

Double-check ✔✔ Apply What You've Learned

a. $k + 7 = -3$ **b.** $3 = \partial + 6$

c. $z + -9 = 46$ **d.** $11 = l + -8$

e. On the first week of the month, Julianne had $17 in her backpack. At the end of the month, she owed her friend Sue $7. How much did Julianne spend over the course of the month?

addition equation.

How does this subject apply to real life?

 **Plan**

After you preview, make a plan for reading. Use the strategy of visualizing and listing the steps you will need to learn to help you get *more* from a math chapter.

• **Visualizing and thinking aloud helps you take an abstract idea (the math problem) and turn it into a concrete drawing or explanation.**

During Reading

D **Read with a Purpose**

Remember that your purpose for reading is to learn the skills taught in the chapter.

Directions: Now do a careful reading of the sample math chapter. Make notes on the stickies.

Using the Strategy

Visualizing means drawing a diagram or sketch of the problem. Listing the steps will break down your task to its simplest parts.

Directions: Reread the practice problem from the math chapter. Draw a sketch and then write down all the things you will have to do to solve it.

Sample Problem

On the first week of the month, Julianne had $17 in her backpack. At the end of the month, she owed her friend Sue $7. How much did Julianne spend over the course of the month?

Visualizing

Listing the Steps

....

....

....

....

....

....

....

Understanding How Math Textbooks Are Organized

Most chapters in math textbooks open with a study guide or goals box that lists key terms and objectives. For example:

Goals

- Learn how to solve addition equations.
- Understand how to use addition equations to solve real-life problems.

Key Terms

addition equation

variable

After you finish your careful reading of the chapter, return to the study guide on the opening page. Be sure you've met each goal and learned each term.

Directions: Answer these questions using the notes you made while reading the math text.

What is an addition equation?

What is a variable?

How do you solve an addition equation?

How might you use an addition equation to solve a real-life problem?

NAME ....

FOR USE WITH PAGES 100–111

 **Connect**

Math will feel more relevant to your life if you turn abstract problems into real-life ones.

- **Making a connection between a math problem and the real world can make the problem easier to solve.**

Directions: Review the chart at the top of page 109 in the *Reader's Handbook*. Then, write a real-life problem for the abstract problem in the chart below.

Textbooks *(side tab)*

◀ **Real-life Problem**

Abstract Problem	Real-life Problem
700 + x = −300	

After Reading

Always take a moment to think about what you've learned.

F **Pause and Reflect**

Return to your reading purpose. Ask yourself, "Have I met my purpose?" and "Did I learn what this chapter was trying to teach me?"

- **After you finish reading, ask yourself, "How well did I meet my purpose?"**

Directions: Answer these questions about the addition equations chapter.

◀ **Looking Back**

Do I understand the key terms?
Do I know how to solve an addition equation?
Are the sample problems clear to me?
Can I complete the exercises?
Would I do well on a test that covered this material?

Reread

Think about key strategies you learned from the chapter. If you don't understand one of them, you'll need to do some reviewing.

> • **Use the rereading strategy of note-taking to help you remember information in the chapter.**

Directions: Read the concepts in the left-hand column. Write your own example of the concept in the right-hand column.

Key Word Notes

Key Words and Concepts	Examples
equation	
variable	
addition equation	
subtracting the same number	
from both sides of the equation	

 Remember

Keep in mind that math concepts build on each other. Don't leave a chapter until you're certain you'll remember what you've learned.

> • **A practice test can help you remember the important parts of a reading.**

Directions: Write a practice test on solving addition equations. Then, write the answer key.

Practice Test

_____

_____

_____

Answer Key

_____

Focus on Foreign Language

Reading a foreign language text is not that much different from reading a science or history text. The same reading process and reading tools apply.

Step 1 Read the paragraph.

Begin with an active reading of the textbook page. Make notes as you go.

Directions: Read the following page from a Spanish text. Make notes on the sticky.

Comparativos y Superlativos

➤➤Most of the adjectives you have learned so far can be used to compare things or people in this way:
El hombre es importante.
El hombre es más importante que el alcalde.

➤➤To say that something or someone is the "most" or "best," use *de* or *del:*
El hombre es la persona más importante de la ciudad.
Mi pueblo es lo más bonito del mundo.

Ejercicios
El modelo
Lila es fuerte. (Yo)
Yo soy más fuerte que Lila.

Cambie las frases según el modelo.
1. El perro blanco es gordo. (flaco)
2. Guillermo es buen médico. (mal)
3. Señora Diego es buena cocinera. (la mejor)

Objectives
Understand how comparisons are made in Spanish.

NOTA
Use *de* when the object is feminine and *del* when the object is masculine. Remember that *lo* means "the one who" or "the one that" and describes the subject.

What is the textbook page about?
....
....
....
....
....

Step 2 Organize what you've learned.

Next, make a quick organizer to show what you've learned. This will help you process and remember the information.

Directions: Record your notes from the reading in this Web.

Web

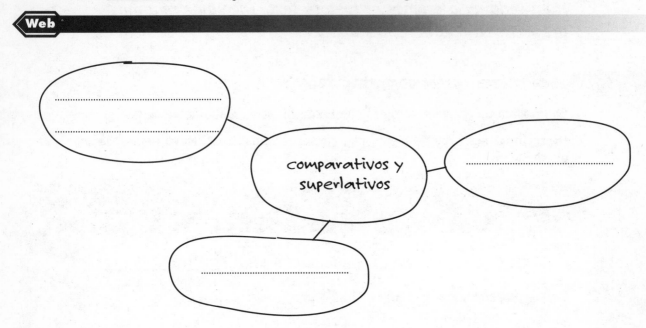

comparativos y superlativos

Step 3 Commit what you've learned to memory.

Memorizing what you've read is an important part of learning a foreign language. Creating a study test can help.

Directions: Read the review tips on page 117 of the *Reader's Handbook*. Then write four test questions for the Spanish page you read.

Sample Test

1. ....

....

2. ....

....

3. ....

....

4. ....

....

Focus on Science Concepts

Much of what you read in a science text will involve concepts. The reading process can help you master the information and techniques.

Step 1 Learn key terms.

To understand a science concept, you must first learn the key terms.

Directions: Look at the rock cycle diagram below. Write key words in the word bank on page 50. Then, use a dictionary to define each term.

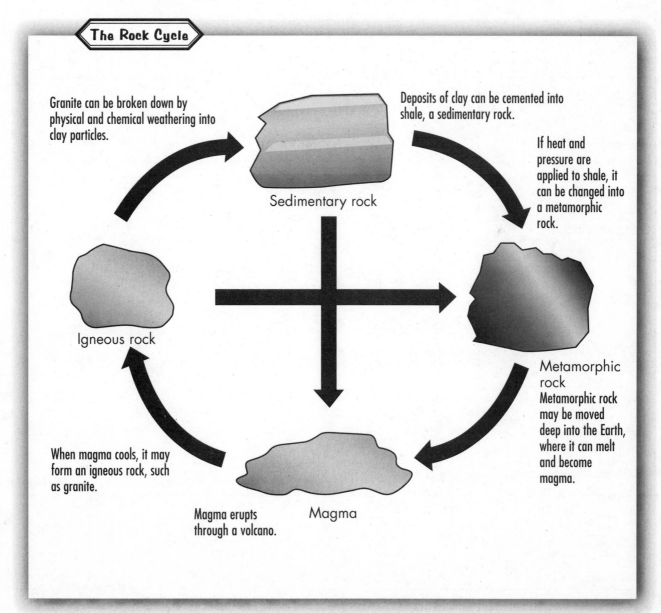

The Rock Cycle

Granite can be broken down by physical and chemical weathering into clay particles.

Deposits of clay can be cemented into shale, a sedimentary rock.

If heat and pressure are applied to shale, it can be changed into a metamorphic rock.

Sedimentary rock

Igneous rock

Metamorphic rock
Metamorphic rock may be moved deep into the Earth, where it can melt and become magma.

When magma cools, it may form an igneous rock, such as granite.

Magma erupts through a volcano.

Magma

NAME ....

FOR USE WITH PAGES 119–124

Word Bank

Word	Definition
igneous rocks	
weathering	
erosion	
sedimentary rocks	
metamorphic rocks	
magma	

Step 2 Track steps in the process.

Now, figure out how the process works.

Directions: Write the steps of the rock cycle here. Use key terms from your word bank.

◀ **Flow Chart**

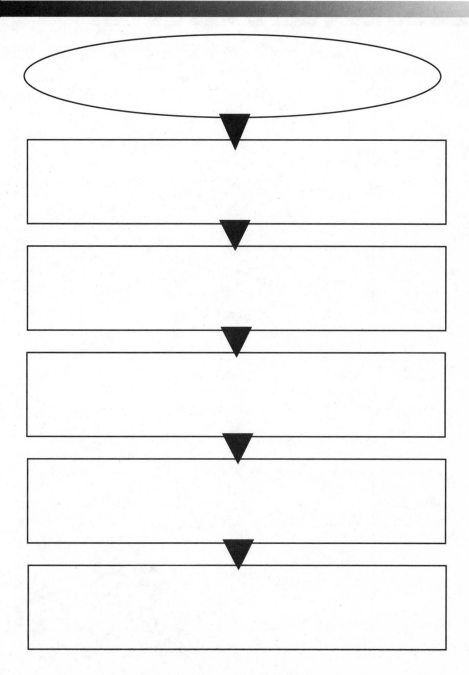

Step 3 Retell the process.

Finish by describing the process to a friend. This will help you retain what you've learned.

Directions: Retell the steps in the rock cycle on the lines below. Refer to your notes as needed.

◄ **Retelling**

....

....

....

....

....

....

....

....

....

....

....

....

....

....

Focus on Study Questions

Reading a question carefully is an important first step in answering it. Careful readers know that most questions require two or even three readings.

Step 1 Read the question two times or more.

Begin by reading the question at least twice. Find the key words.

Directions: Read this sample question. Highlight the key words.

> **Sample Question**
>
> Summarize the Supreme Court's ruling in *Plessy* v. *Ferguson*. Then, explain the effect it had on African-American children in the South.

Step 2 Choose a strategy.

Next, choose a strategy that can help you answer the question. In many cases, visualizing and thinking aloud will be your best choices.

Directions: On the lines below, explain what you need to do to answer the *Plessy* v. *Ferguson* question. Then, name the strategy you'll use.

To answer the question, I will ....

....

....

....

Strategy I'll use: because ....

....

....

....

Step 3 Answer the question.

Next, use the strategy to answer the question.

Directions: Write a Think Aloud for the *Plessy* v. *Ferguson* question.

◁ **Think Aloud**

Partner: ....

....

....

....

....

....

....

....

....

....

....

....

....

....

....

....

Step 4 Check your answer.

The last step is to check your work. Reread the question and then ask yourself, "Is my answer reasonable?"

Directions: Reread your answer. Exchange books with a partner. Read your partner's writing and make comments in the margin. Check to be sure that your partner's answer is reasonable.

Focus on Word Problems

Have you noticed that the word problems in math class seem to be getting trickier and trickier? But even the hardest problems are solved in basically the same way. Using a four-step reading plan will help eliminate the confusion.

Step 1 Read the problem.

The first step in solving a word problem is to read it carefully.

Directions: Read the following word problem. Highlight key words. Make notes on the sticky.

> **Sample Question**
>
> The daily noontime temperature in Detroit during the first week of March was 5° F. On Saturday and Sunday, the noontime temperature dropped to –5°F. What was the average daily noontime temperature for that first week in March? Round to the nearest degree.

The topic is: ....
....

The given is: ....
....
....

I need to find: ....
....

Step 2 Choose a strategy.

The best strategy to use with word problems is visualizing and thinking aloud.

Directions: Make a sketch that shows the daily temperature problem.

Sketch

Step 3 Solve.

Use your strategy to solve the problem.

Directions: Write a numerical expression for the problem. Then solve it.

....

....

....

....

Step 4 Check.

Your last step is to check your work. Is your answer reasonable?

Directions: Write a Think Aloud that shows how you solved the problem.

◀ Think Aloud

....

....

....

....

....

....

....

....

....

....

....

Reading a Personal Essay

A personal essay is informal and can deal with any subject. In most personal essays, the writer opens with an interesting autobiographical story. Later in the essay, the writer explains a point, insight, or lesson that can be taken from that story.

Before Reading

Practice reading and responding to a personal essay here. Use the reading process and the strategy of outlining to help you read an essay by Max Beerbohm.

A Set a Purpose

Your purpose will be to find the subject and main idea of the essay. In addition, you'll want to decide how you feel about the essayist's main idea.

- **To set your purpose, ask questions about the essay's subject and main idea.**

Directions: Write three purpose questions for the essay "Going Out for a Walk."

Purpose question 1: ....

Purpose question 2: ....

Purpose question 3: ....

B Preview

Always preview an essay before you begin reading. Pay careful attention to these key parts:

◄ **Preview Checklist**

- ☐ the title and author
- ☐ the first and last paragraphs
- ☐ any repeated words or phrases
- ☐ any key words or words in boldface or italics

Nonfiction

Directions: Preview "Going Out for a Walk." Write your preview notes on this Web. Add more boxes if you need to.

Web

Author's name:

Essay subject:

Repeated words:

"Going Out for a Walk"

Background information:

First paragraph details:

Last paragraph details:

from "Going Out for a Walk" by Max Beerbohm

Max Beerbohm (1872-1956) was a British essayist who was famous for his witty criticism of anything that was pretentious or absurd in English society. In this essay, which was published in 1919, Beerbohm pokes fun at men and women who go out walking when they have absolutely nowhere to go.

It is a fact that not once in all my life have I gone out for a walk. I have been taken out for walks; but that is another matter. Even while I trotted prattling by my nurse's side I regretted the good old days when I had, and wasn't, a perambulator. When I grew up it seemed to me that the one advantage of living in London was that nobody ever wanted me to come out for a walk. London's very drawbacks—its endless noise and hustle, its smoky air, the squalor ambushed everywhere in it—assured this one immunity. Whenever I was with friends in the country, I knew that at any moment, unless rain were actually falling, some man might suddenly say "Come out for a walk!" in that sharp imperative tone which he would not dream of using in any other connection.

Stop and Organize

Make some notes in the "Introduction" section of your Outline on page 61.

People seem to think there is something inherently noble and virtuous in the desire to go for a walk. Anyone thus desirous feels that he has a right to impose his will on whomever he sees comfortably settled in an arm-chair, reading. It is easy to say simply "No" to an old friend. In the case of a mere acquaintance one wants some excuse. "I wish I could, but"—nothing ever occurs to me except "I have some letters to write." This formula is unsatisfactory in three ways. (1) It isn't believed. (2) It compels you to rise from your chair, go to the writing-table, and sit improvising a letter to somebody until the walkmonger (just not daring to call you liar and hypocrite) shall have lumbered out of the room. (3) It won't operate on Sunday mornings. "There's no post out till this evening" clinches the matter; and you may as well go quietly.

Stop and Organize

Make some notes in the "Body" section of your Outline on page 61.

Walking for walking's sake may be as highly laudable and exemplary a thing as it is held to be by those who practice it. My objection to it is that it stops the brain.

from "Going Out for a Walk" by Max Beerbohm

Many a man has professed to me that his brain never works so well as when he is swinging along the high road or over hill and dale. This boast is not confirmed by my memory of anybody who on a Sunday morning has forced me to partake of his adventure. Experience teaches me that whatever a fellow-guest may have of power to instruct or to amuse when he is sitting on a chair, or standing on a hearth-rug, quickly leaves him when he takes one out for a walk. The ideas that came so thick and fast to him in any room, where are they now? where that encyclopaedic knowledge which he bore so lightly? where the kindling fancy that played like summer lightning over any topic that was started? The man's face that was so mobile is set now; gone is the light from his fine eyes. He says that A. (our host) is a thoroughly good fellow. Fifty yards further on, he adds that A. is one of the best fellows he has ever met. We tramp another furlong or so, and he says that Mrs. A. is a charming woman. Presently he adds that she is one of the most charming women he has ever known. We pass an inn. He reads vapidly aloud to me: "The King's Arms. Licensed to sell Ales and Spirits." I foresee that during the rest of the walk he will read aloud any inscription that occurs. We pass a milestone. He points at it with his stick, and says "Uxminster. 11 Miles." We turn a sharp corner at the foot of a hill. He points at the wall, and says "Drive Slowly." I see far ahead, on the other side of the hedge bordering the high road, a small notice-board. He sees it too. He keeps his eye on it. And in due course "Trespassers," he says, "Will Be Prosecuted." Poor man!—mentally a wreck. . . .

Stop and Organize
Make some more notes in the "Body" section of your Outline on page 61.

. . . Such as it is, this essay was composed in the course of a walk, this morning. I am not one of those extremists who must have a vehicle to every destination. I never go out of my way, as it were, to avoid exercise. I take it as it comes, and take it in good part. That valetudinarians[1] are always chattering about it, and indulging in it to excess, is no reason for despising it. I am inclined to think that in moderation it is rather good for one, physically. But, pending a time when no people wish me to go and see them, and I have no wish to go and see anyone, and there is nothing whatever for me to do off my own premises, I never will go out for a walk.

Stop and Organize
Make some notes in the "Conclusion" section of you Outline on page 61.

1. **valetudinarians**—sickly persons

 **Plan**

Now, make a reading plan that will help you meet your purpose. Many readers find that the strategy of outlining can help you get *more* from an essay.

> • **Outlining forces you to decide what information is the most important in an essay.**

During Reading

Watch for the three major parts of the essay: the introduction, the body, and the conclusion. If you need help with these terms, see page 159 of the *Reader's Handbook.*

D Read with a Purpose

Keep your purpose questions in mind as you read. Remember that you are looking for the topic and main idea of the essay.

Directions: Do a careful reading of "Going Out for a Walk." Make notes on this Outline as you read.

Outline

I. Introduction

   A. Detail:

   B. Detail:

   C. Detail:

II. Body

   A. Detail:

   B. Detail:

   C. Detail:

III. Conclusion

   A. Detail:

   B. Detail:

   C. Detail:

Nonfiction

Understanding How Essays **Are Organized**

Most personal essays are organized in a funnel pattern.

- **In a funnel pattern, the writer builds toward the main idea.**

Directions: Complete this organizer with information from "Going Out for a Walk."

Name the topic here.

....

List details that relate to the topic here.

....

....

....

Write a key detail from the conclusion here.

....

....

....

Write the essayist's main idea here.

....

....

....

....

E Connect

Remember that part of your reading purpose involves deciding how you feel about the essayist's main idea.

- **Connect to an essay by recording your thoughts and feelings about the main idea.**

Directions: Read this sentence from the essay. Write your reaction to it on the sticky.

But, pending a time when no people wish me to go and see them, and I have no wish to go and see anyone, and there is nothing whatever for me to do off my own premises, I never will go out for a walk.

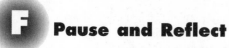

When you finish reading, take a moment or two to think about what the author has said.

F Pause and Reflect

Ask yourself questions about the essay and your purpose for reading.

> • **After you finish an essay, ask yourself, "How well did I meet my purpose?"**

<u>Directions:</u> Answer these questions about "Going Out for a Walk."

> **Looking Back**

What is the subject of the essay?

....

....

....

What does the author say about the subject?

....

....

....

How do you feel about the author's message?

....

....

....

Do you feel you've met your reading purpose?

....

....

....

G Reread

The strategy of questioning the author can help you if you're not sure you've fully understood the essay.

> • **A powerful rereading strategy to use is questioning the author.**

Directions: Write three questions that you would like to ask Max Beerbohm. Then, write the answers you think he might have given.

Question 1: ....

....

Beerbohm's answer: ....

....

Question 2: ....

....

Beerbohm's answer: ....

....

Question 3: ....

....

Beerbohm's answer: ....

....

 H **Remember**

Completing an organizer can help you remember what you've just read.

• **A Main Idea Organizer can help you pull together everything you've learned.**

Directions: Complete this organizer using notes from your reading.

Topic:		
Main Idea:		
Detail 1	Detail 2	Detail 3

Reading an Editorial

The purpose of most editorials is to advance an argument or comment on the important issues of the day. Your job as the reader is to understand and evaluate the assertions the writer makes.

Before Reading

Practice reading and responding to an editorial here. Employing the strategy of questioning the author will help you fully grasp the author's points.

A Set a Purpose

Your purpose is to understand the author's viewpoint, evaluate how persuasively the point is supported, and decide how you feel about it.

• To set your purpose, ask questions about the viewpoint and support.

Directions: Write your purpose for reading the editorial "A Modest Rebuttal" on the lines below.

Purpose question #1 ....

Purpose question #2 ....

Purpose question #3 ....

B Preview

Your main goal when previewing is to get a sense of the subject of the editorial. Take a close look at the items on this checklist:

▶ **Preview Checklist**

☐ the headline and date

☐ any repeated words

☐ the first and last paragraphs

☐ the writer's assertion

Directions: Preview "A Modest Rebuttal." Write your preview notes on the chart below. Then infer what you think is the topic of the editorial.

Preview Chart

Items Previewed	My Notes
the headline	
the date	
the first paragraph	
the last paragraph	
repeated words and phrases	

I think the editorial is going to be about:

....

The Valley High School Times

Home of the Eagles

Volume 42: Issue 14	January 17

A Modest Rebuttal

Every year, right around the beginning of September, school district officials, teachers, and parents stir themselves up into a frenzy of debate and handwringing. The issue that is riling our role models? Is it poverty in our cities or homelessness on our streets? Is it landfills filling, factories polluting, or eagles expiring?

Actually, it's none of these things. The issue that's causing all the wailing and worrying is a debate over junk food. To be more specific—it is whether or not junk food should be served in the high school cafeteria.

Stop and Organize

Why does the author begin this way? Make notes on your Double-entry Journal on page 69.

"A Modest Rebuttal"

To many, the question of whether our school should be allowed to "peddle" junk food is all but unanswerable. School nurses say no to burgers and fries; cafeteria workers say yes. Parents say no; kids say yes. It's the unending debate—or so it seems.

In reality, a little research can go a long way toward answering this question and resolving the debate. A quick reading of *The California Journal of Nutrition* or a few minutes' research on the Internet yields a wealth of nutritional data that even Betty Crocker could not dispute.

The fact of the matter is, serving junk food in the school cafeteria has little or no effect on the overall health of students and can actually *benefit* students by encouraging them to make healthier meal choices at other times during the day.

Stop and Organize
What point is the author making here? Make notes on your Double-entry Journal on page 69.

Last year, a group of local nutritionists, led by Dr. Dionne Landers of City Hospital, surveyed twelve different high schools in our state. All twelve of these schools had just recently begun serving junk food in their cafeterias.

Each school participating in the survey was asked to instruct students to keep a food journal of everything they ate for lunch and dinner in the month of September.

At the end of the month, Landers and her group began reading the students' food journals. "What we found in these journals surprised us very much," Dr. Landers reports. "We expected to learn that kids were choosing junk food five lunches a week, and then going home and eating basically the same thing for dinner."

Instead, Landers and her colleagues learned that the opposite was true. Their findings indicated that students who ate a junk food lunch tended to eat a well-balanced dinner. On the other hand, students who chose the cafeteria special—which by law must meet federal nutritional requirements for teens—tended to eat a "junky" dinner.

Stop and Organize
How does this information support the author's assertion? Make notes on your Double-entry Journal on page 69.

"Basically what we were seeing is that those students who ate burgers and fries for lunch would compensate by eating pasta and a salad for dinner. They did this either consciously or unconsciously. Students, however, who chose the cafeteria special for lunch tended to opt for burgers and fries for dinner."

After the survey was finished, Landers and her group published their report and filed it with the state department of education. What the report says, in essence, is that teens who are

"A Modest Rebuttal"

given plenty of choices end up meeting their daily nutritional requirement without even realizing it.

Critics of the plan to serve burgers, fries, and pizza in our school cafeteria should take a careful look at Landers's data. Their charge that malnutrition

reigns where burger is king is clearly refuted in Landers's report.

The truth of the matter is that if they are given plenty of meal choices, most teens will choose well. So let us have a burger, fries, and soda at lunch, and then it's please pass the broccoli at dinner.

Stop and Organize

What action are readers supposed to take or how are readers supposed to feel as a result of this editorial? Make notes on your Double-entry Journal on page 69.

C Plan

After your preview, make a plan for reading. Choose a strategy that can help you take note of the author's assertions (statements about the topic) and the support for the assertions. An excellent strategy to use is questioning the author.

- **Use the strategy of questioning the author to help you find the writer's assertions and support.**

During Reading

D Read with a Purpose

Keep your purpose in mind as you read. Remember that you want to find out what point the author is making and how he or she supports that point. Asking (and answering) questions can help.

<u>Directions:</u> Do a careful reading of the editorial. Ask questions of the author. Make notes on the following Double-entry Journal.

NAME

◄ **Double-entry Journal**

Questions	My Thoughts
Why does the author begin this way?	
What point is the author making here?	
How does this information support the author's assertion?	
What action are readers supposed to take or how are readers supposed to feel as a result of this editorial?	

Nonfiction

Using the Strategy

After you ask and answer the questions, use a critical reading chart to evaluate the information in the editorial.

Directions: Record your answers to these critical reading questions.

Critical Reading Chart

Questions	My Thoughts
1. What topic is the writer discussing?	
2. How does the writer feel about the topic?	
3. What are the writer's assertions?	
4. How does the writer support the assertions?	
5. What do I think about this topic?	
6. How do my thoughts compare with those of the writer?	

Understanding How Editorials **Are Organized**

Most editorials contain three parts: the writer's assertions, the support, and the recommendation. Very often the parts follow the structure like the one on page 175 of the *Reader's Handbook*.

• **Most editorials contain assertions, support for the assertions, and a recommendation.**

Directions: Record the writer's assertions, support, and recommendation in "A Modest Rebuttal" on this organizer.

◀ Editorial Structure

1. Assertion

....

....

....

Supporting detail

....

....

....

▼

2. Assertion

....

....

Supporting detail

....

....

....

▼

3. Recommendations

....

....

....

....

Nonfiction

E Connect

Connecting to an editorial is important and easy. You react to the author's assertions and compare them to your own experience. Deciding how you feel about the writer's argument is an important part of your reading purpose.

• Connect to an editorial by recording your thoughts and feelings.

<u>Directions:</u> Reread the final two paragraphs of the editorial. Then, make notes on the sticky.

Critics of the plan to serve burgers, fries, and pizza in our school cafeteria should take a careful look at Landers's data. Their charge that malnutrition reigns when burger is king is clearly refuted in Landers's report.

The truth of the matter is that if they are given plenty of meal choices, most teens will choose well. So let us have a burger, fries, and soda at lunch, and then it's please pass the broccoli at dinner.

After Reading

It's not a bad idea to spend a few minutes thinking about an editorial after you finish reading it. After all, you never know when the information you've learned will come in handy.

F Pause and Reflect

Ask yourself questions about the editorial and your purpose for reading.

• After you finish an editorial, ask yourself, "Do I understand the author's ideas and opinions?"

<u>Directions:</u> Answer these questions about "A Modest Rebuttal."

Questions

What is the "modest rebuttal"?

Can you explain how the writer supports the viewpoint?

Do you know how you feel about the editorial?

Reread

Sometimes you may feel you need to reread an editorial. Maybe you want to find out more about the author's viewpoint. Or maybe you'd like to take another look at the author's support for the viewpoint.

• **A powerful rereading strategy to use with an editorial is synthesizing.**

Synthesizing means examining bits of information from a piece of writing and then putting them together to see what they mean.

Directions: Complete this synthesizing chart. Use the notes you made while reading the editorial.

Synthesizing Chart

Editorial	My Thoughts
Topic:	What's my opinion?
What are the author's assertions?	Supporting detail #1
	Supporting detail #2
Supporting detail #1	Supporting detail #3
Supporting detail #2	My conclusion:

Nonfiction

Remember

Good readers remember what they've read. Writing a letter to a friend can help lock the ideas in your head.

- **Writing a letter can help you remember the most important points in an editorial.**

Directions: Write a brief letter to a friend. In your letter, explain the writer's point in "A Modest Rebuttal" and your opinion of it.

Letter

Reading a News Story

Reading a news story is like hunting for shells on the beach. The facts are there, if you know how to find them. The reading process can help.

Before Reading

Here, you'll use the reading process to help you read and understand a news story that was published in 1919.

A Set a Purpose

Begin by setting your purpose. In most cases, your purpose will be to find out answers to these questions: *who, what, where, when, why,* and *how.*

• **To set your purpose, ask *who, what, where, when, why,* and *how* questions about the story's headline.**

<u>**Directions:**</u> Write your purpose for reading "Ghastly Deeds of Race Rioters Told" on the lines below. Then, explain what you already know about the subject.

My purpose question: ....

....

This is what I know about the subject: ....

....

....

....

B Preview

Use your preview time to get a handle on the topic of the article. Pay attention to items on this checklist.

◄ **Preview Checklist**

☐ the headline

☐ the lead

☐ any key words or repeated phrases

Directions: Preview the background information and lead of "Ghastly Deeds of Race Rioters Told." Make notes on this 5 W's and H Organizer.

5 W's and H Organizer

Who	What	Where	When	Why	How

In the spring and summer of 1919, bloody race riots erupted in 22 American cities and towns. The most severe of these took place in Chicago, in late July. The violence began when white beachgoers attacked several black youths who had drifted toward one of the "Whites Only" Lake Michigan beaches. Five days of intense racial violence followed in many parts of the city. A total of 23 African-American and 15 white Chicagoans were killed. More than 500 whites and blacks were badly injured, and thousands were burned out of their homes. The article that follows was written by a reporter for the Chicago Defender. It was published on the fifth and final day of the riots.

Ghastly Deeds of Race Rioters Told

For fully four days this old city has been rocked in a quake of racial antagonism, seared in a blaze of red hate flaming as fiercely as the heat of day— each hour ushering in new stories of slaying, looting, arson, and rape, sending the awful roll of casualties to a grand total of 40 dead and more than 500 wounded, many of them perhaps fatally. A certain madness distinctly indicated in reports of shootings, stabbings, and burning of buildings which literally pour in every minute. Women and children have not been spared. Traffic has been stopped. Phone wires have been cut.

Stores and Offices Shut

Victims lay in every street and vacant lot. Hospitals are filled: 4,000 troops rest in arms, among which are companies of the old Eighth regiment, while the inadequate force of police battles vainly to save the city's honor.

"Ghastly Deeds of Race Rioters Told"

Fear to Care for Bodies

Undertakers on the South Side refused to accept the bodies of white victims. White undertakers refused to accept black victims. Both for the same reason. They feared the vengeance of the mobs without.

Every little while bodies were found in some street, alley, or vacant lot—and no one sought to care for them. Patrols were unable to accommodate them because they were being used in rushing live victims to hospitals. Some victims were dragged to a mob's "No Man's Land" and dropped.

The telephone wires in the raging districts were cut in many places by the rioters, as it became difficult to estimate the number of dead victims. . . .

Monday Sees "Reign of Terror"

Following the Sunday affray, the red tongues had blabbed their fill, and Monday morning found the thoroughfares in the white neighborhoods throated with a sea of humans—everywhere—some armed with guns, bricks, clubs, and an oath. The presence of a black face in their vicinity was a signal for a carnival of death, and before any aid could reach the poor, unfortunate one his body reposed in some kindly gutter, his brains spilled over a dirty pavement. Some of the victims were chased, caught, and dragged into alleys and lots, where they were left for dead. In all parts of the city, white mobs dragged from surface cars, black passengers wholly ignorant of any

trouble, and set upon them. An unidentified man, young woman, and a 3-month old baby were found dead on the street at the intersection of 47th Street and Wentworth Avenue. She had attempted to board a car there when the mob seized her, beat her, slashed her body into ribbons, and beat the baby's brains out against a telegraph pole. . . . All the time this was happening, several policemen were in the crowd, but did not make any attempt to make rescue until too late.

Stop and Record

What facts does the reporter give? What opinions does he give? Record them on your Critical Reading Chart on page 80.

Kill Scores Coming from Yards

Rioters operating in the vicinity of the stockyards, which lies in the heart of white residences west of Halsted Street, attacked scores of workers—women and men alike returning from work. Stories of these outrages began to flutter into the black vicinities and hysterical men harangued their fellows to avenge the killings—and soon they, infected with the insanity of the mob, rushed through the streets, drove high powered motorcars, or waited for streetcars which they attacked with gunfire and stones. Shortly after noon all traffic south of 22nd Street and north of 55th Street, west of Cottage Grove Avenue and east of Wentworth Avenue, was stopped with the exception

"Ghastly Deeds of Race Rioters Told"

of trolley cars. Whites who entered this zone were set upon with unmeasurable fury.

Policemen employed in the disturbed sections were wholly unable to handle the situation. When one did attempt to carry out his duty he was beaten and his gun taken from him. The fury of the mob could not be abated. Mounted police were employed, but to no avail.

35th Vortex of Night's Rioting

With the approach of darkness the rioting gave prospects of being continued throughout the night. Whites boarded the platforms and shot through the windows of the trains at passengers. Some of the passengers alighting themselves from cars were thrown from the elevated structure, suffering broken legs, fractured skulls, and death.

The block between State Street and Wabash Avenue on East 35th Street was the scene of probably the most shooting and rioting of the evening and a pitched battle ensued between the police, whites, and blacks.

The trouble climaxed when white occupants of the Angelus apartments began firing shots and throwing missiles from their windows. One man was shot through the head, but before his name could be secured he was spirited away. The attack developed a hysterical battling fervor and the mob charged the building and the battle was on.

Police were shot. Whites were seen to tumble out of automobiles, from doorways, and other places, wounded or suffering from bruises inflicted by

gunshots, stones, or bricks. A reign of terror literally ensued. Automobiles were stopped, occupants beaten, and machines wrecked. Streetcars operating in 35th Street were wrecked as well as north and south bound State Street cars. Windows were shattered and white occupants beaten. . . .

Stores Looted: Homes Burned

Tiring of street fights, rioters turned to burning and looting. This was truly a sleepless night and a résumé of the day's happenings nourished an inclination for renewed hostilities from another angle. The homes of blacks isolated in white neighborhoods were burned to the ground and the owners and occupants beaten and thrown unconscious in the smoldering embers. Meanwhile rioters in the "black belt" smashed windows and looted the shops of white merchants on State Street.

Other rioters, manning high powered cars and armed, flitted up and down the darkened streets, chancing shots at fleeing whites on the street and those riding in streetcars.

Toward midnight quiet reigned along State Street under the vigilance of 400 policemen and scores of uniformed men of the 8th Regiment.

Stop and Record

How does the reporter feel about the riots? Make notes in the main idea section of your Critical Reading Chart on page 80.

"Ghastly Deeds of Race Rioters Told"

Rioting Extends Into Loop

Tuesday dawned sorrowing with a death toll of 20 dead and 300 injured. . . . But hell was yet to break loose, and by fate I was destined to be present. It occurred at Wabash Avenue and 35th Street at 8:10 o'clock at night, when over fifty policemen, mounted and on foot, while in the attempt to disperse a mob that was playing havoc with every white face, drew their revolvers and showered bullets into the crowd. The officers' guns barked for fully ten minutes. Seeing no way to escape and at the same time thinking of the obituary column, I immediately decided that my best move was to fall face downward to the pavement and remain there 'til the air cleared. This I did at the expense of a perfectly new straw bonnet. But it was worth it.

Stop and Record

Are the reporter's sources authoritative and reliable? Make notes on your Critical Reading Chart on page 80.

Four Wounded

During the reign of terror four citizens fell wounded; one a woman. She voiced her distress after a bullet had pierced her left shoulder. A man of slender proportions stumbled over my body in the hurried attempt to escape and plunged head first into the ground. A stream of blood gushed from a wound in the back of his neck. The bullet from an officer's revolver had found its mark. Blood from his fatal wound trickled down the pavement until it had reached me and heated corpuscles bathed my left cheek as I awaited the cessation of hostilities. The pavement about me was literally covered with splintered glass which had been torn from a laundry window by the fusillade of shots, and several times I was tempted to brush the broken fragments from my back, where some had fallen, but I dreaded making a move. I had a reason. It was a case of eventuality, but not now.

Beads of perspiration rolled off my forehead as a bullet passed over the back of my coat, burning a path near the collar as it sped on its deathly mission. I arose reluctantly as a cop yelled: "Get up, everybody." He said it in the 200-point type we use on the front page of extras. His command was obeyed.

The wounded were whisked away in automobiles to nearby hospitals for treatment. Shortly after the guns had ceased firing the telephone on the managing editor's desk at the office tinkled. He answered.

"Have you heard of the shooting at 35th and Wabash Avenue?" queried a mellow tone voice on the other end. The rejoinder came, evidenced in clear tones: "Yes, madam, a *Defender* reporter was passing."

Nonfiction

Plan

Now that you have a general idea of the topic of the article, make a plan. What strategy will help you meet your purpose for reading?

• **Use the strategy of reading critically with newspaper articles.**

Reading critically means looking at all of the facts presented and deciding how believable they are. Focus on which facts you know you can believe.

During Reading

D Read with a Purpose

Now you're ready for a careful reading of the article.

Directions: Read "Ghastly Deeds of Race Rioters Told." As you read, write down key facts and opinions on the following Critical Reading Chart.

Critical Reading Chart

Key Facts	Key Opinions

Using the Strategy

Reading critically means understanding the facts presented. As the article is a long one, you'll need to sift through many facts to get to the most important ones.

Directions: Look at your notes and then complete this chart. When you are done, answer the question below.

Key Facts Chart

Write three key facts about the riot here:

1.

2.

3.

Write three key facts about the African-American rioters here:

1.

2.

3.

Write three key facts about the white rioters here:

1.

2.

3.

Write your conclusions here:

Are the reporter's sources reliable?

Understanding How News Stories Are Organized

In a news story, you'll find an overview of the most important facts in the lead.

- **The lead tells you *who, what, where, when, why,* and *how.***

Directions: Reread the *Chicago Defender* lead. Highlight clues about *who, what,* and *where.* Circle clues about *when, why,* and *how.*

> For fully four days this old city has been rocked in a quake of racial antagonism, seared in a blaze of red hate flaming as fiercely as the heat of day—each hour ushering in new stories of slaying, looting, arson, and rape, sending the awful roll of casualties to a grand total of 40 dead and more than 500 wounded, many of them perhaps fatally. A certain madness distinctly indicated in reports of shootings, stabbings, and burning of buildings which literally pour in every minute. Women and children have not been spared. Traffic has been stopped. Phone wires have been cut.

Connect

Think about how the information in a news story applies to you. This can make the story more interesting and meaningful.

- **To connect to a news story, ask yourself, "How does this apply to me?" or "What else do I know about this subject?"**

Directions: Answer this question about the *Chicago Defender* article.

What else do you know about the Chicago race riots?

....

....

....

....

....

....

....

....

After Reading

After you finish a news story, reflect on what you've learned.

 F ## Pause and Reflect

At this point, you'll want to return to your original reading purpose.

- **Ask yourself, "Can I answer *who, what, where, when, why,* and *how?*"**

Directions: Answer these questions about the *Chicago Defender* story.

Questions

Decide	Yes	No
I can answer <u>who</u>, <u>what</u>, <u>where</u>, <u>when</u>, <u>why</u>, and <u>how</u> questions.		
I know which details are facts and which are opinions.		
I understand the article's main idea.		
I can find three details the reporter uses to support the main idea.		

 G ## Reread

If you haven't met your reading purpose, you need to return to the text.

- **A powerful rereading strategy to use with a news story is summarizing.**

Directions: Write Summary Notes for the story you read.

Summary Notes

Article headline:
Subject:
Author's main idea:
Supporting detail #1
Supporting detail #2
Supporting detail #3

Nonfiction

Remember

Remembering the key facts of a news story can help you speak
knowledgeably about the subject.

• **Create a graphic organizer that will help you remember facts and
details from the story.**

Directions: Write the causes of the Chicago race riots in the box on the left.
Then, write two or more effects of the riots.

Cause-Effect Organizer

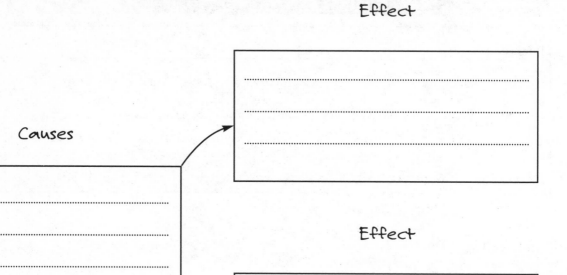

Effect

Causes

Effect

Reading a

A biography is the story of a person's life. Most biographers write with two goals in mind: to tell an interesting story and to create an impression of what the person was really like.

Before Reading

The reading process and strategy of looking for cause and effect can help you get more from every biography you read. Practice here with an excerpt from a biography about the circus impresario P. T. Barnum.

 ### A Set a Purpose

Your primary purpose when reading a biography is to find out as much as you can about the subject and his or her life. Your secondary purpose is to form your own impression of the subject.

• **To set your purpose, ask questions about the biographical subject.**

Directions: Write your purpose for reading a biography about P. T. Barnum. Then, explain what you already know about him.

My purpose: ....

....

Here's what I already know about P. T. Barnum: ....

....

 ### B Preview

Preview a biography by examining the front and back covers and table of contents. Look for important information about the subject.

Directions: Preview *The Life of Phineas Taylor Barnum*. Make notes on the stickies as you preview.

Nonfiction

Back Cover

Meet P. T. Barnum—the greatest American entertainer of all time . . .

To many, Phineas Taylor Barnum was the embodiment of the American Dream. Working on the principle that even the most refined audiences loved to be shocked senseless, Barnum presented to a captive world a series of unforgettable exhibits, including:

• Joice Heith, the 161-year-old woman;

• Chang and Eng, the world's "first Siamese twins";

• the Feejee Mermaid, a woman with the body of a fish;

• and "General" Tom Thumb, the world's tiniest soldier.

Throughout his life, Barnum's drive to succeed was powered by his love of money and his craving to be famous. Here is the biography of the man who was himself "The Greatest Show on Earth."

Important facts about the biographical subject:

Front Cover

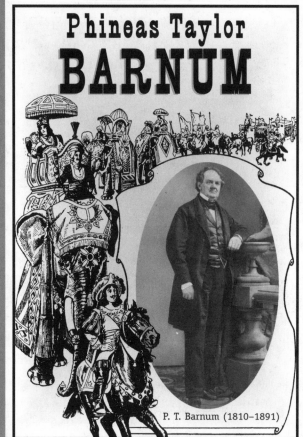

The Life of

Phineas Taylor BARNUM

P. T. Barnum (1810–1891)

by Joel Benton

The subject of the biography is

What is the main time period of the biography?

Plan

After your preview, make a reading plan. Choose a strategy that can help you understand the key events of the subject's life.

> **• Use the strategy of looking for cause and effect to help you understand the effect of the subject's life experiences.**

During Reading

D Read with a Purpose

Keep track of key events in the subject's life and how they affected him or her.

Directions: Do a careful reading of the excerpt from the Barnum biography. Make notes on the Cause-Effect Organizer on page 90.

---

from *The Life of Phineas Taylor Barnum* by Joel Benton

Among the names of great Americans of the nineteenth century, there is scarcely one more familiar to the world than that of the subject of this biography. There are those that stand for higher achievement in literature, science and art, in public life and in the business world. There is none that stands for more notable success in his chosen line, none that recalls more memories of wholesome entertainment, none that is more invested with the fragrance of kindliness and true humanity. His career was, in a large sense, typical of genuine Americanism, of its enterprise and pluck, of its indomitable will and unfailing courage, of its shrewdness, audacity and unerring instinct for success.

Like so many of his famous compatriots, Phineas Taylor Barnum came of good old New England stock. His ancestors were among the builders of the colonies of Massachusetts and Connecticut. His father's father, Ephraim Barnum, was a captain in the War of the Revolution and was distinguished for his valor and for his fervent patriotism. His mother's father, Phineas Taylor, was locally noted as a wag and practical joker. His father, Philo Barnum, was in turn a tailor, a farmer, a storekeeper, and a country tavern keeper and was not particularly prosperous in any of these callings.

Philo Barnum and his wife, Irena Taylor, lived at Bethel, Connecticut, and there, on July 5, 1810, their first child was born. He was named Phineas Taylor Barnum, after his maternal grandfather; and the latter, in return for the compliment, bestowed upon his first grandchild at his christening the title-deeds of a "landed estate," five acres in extent, known as Ivy Island, and situated in that part of Bethel known as the "Plum Trees."

from *The Life of Phineas Taylor Barnum* by Joel Benton

In his early years the boy led the life of the average New England farmer's son of that period. He drove the cows to and from the pasture, shelled corn, weeded the garden, and "did up chores." As he grew older he rode the horse in plowing corn, raked hay, wielded the shovel and the hoe, and chopped wood. At six years old he began to go to school—the typical district school. "The first date," he once said, "I remember inscribing upon my writing-book was 1818." The ferule, or the birch-rod, was in those days the assistant schoolmaster, and young Barnum made its acquaintance. He was, however, an apt and ready scholar, particularly excelling in mathematics. One night, when he was ten years old, he was called out of bed by his teacher, who had made a wager with a neighbor that Barnum could calculate the number of feet in a load of wood in five minutes. Barnum did it in less than two minutes, to the delight of his teacher and the astonishment of the neighbor.

At an early age he manifested a strong development of the good old Yankee organ of acquisitiveness. Before he was five years old he had begun to hoard pennies and "fourpences," and at six years old he was able to exchange his copper bits for a whole silver dollar, the possession of which made him feel richer than he ever felt afterward in all his life. Nor did he lay the dollar away in a napkin, but used it in business to gain more. He would get ten cents a day for riding a horse before the plow, and he would add it to his capital. On holidays other boys spent all their savings, but not so he. Such days were to him opportunities for gain, not for squandering. At the fair or training of troops, or other festivity, he would peddle candy and cakes, home-made, or sometimes cherry rum, and by the end of the day would be a dollar or two richer than at its beginning. "By the time I was twelve years old," he tells us, "I was the owner of a sheep and a calf, and should soon, no doubt, have become a small Croesus had not my father kindly permitted me to purchase my own clothing, which somewhat reduced my little store."

At ten years of age, realizing himself to be a "landed proprietor" through the christening gift of his waggish grandsire, young Barnum set out to survey his estate, which he had not yet seen. He had heard much of "Ivy Island." His grandfather had often, in the presence of the neighbors, spoken of him as the richest child in the town, since he owned the whole of Ivy Island, the richest farm in the State. His parents hoped he would use his wealth wisely, and "do something for the family" when he entered upon the possession of it; and the neighbors were fearful lest he should grow too proud to associate with their children.

The boy took all this in good faith, and his eager curiosity to behold his estate was greatly increased, and he asked his father to let him go thither. "At last," says Barnum, "he promised I should do so in a few days, as we should be getting some hay near 'Ivy Island.' The wished-for day arrived, and my father told me that as we were to mow an adjoining meadow, I might visit my property in company with the hired man during the 'nooning.' My grandfather reminded me that it was to his bounty I was indebted

◇ from *The Life of Phineas Taylor Barnum* by Joel Benton ◇

for this wealth, and that had not my name been Phineas I might never have been proprietor of 'Ivy Island.' To this my mother added:

"'Now, Taylor, don't become so excited when you see your property as to let your joy make you sick, for remember, rich as you are, that it will be eleven years before you can come into possession of your fortune.'

"She added much more good advice, to all of which I promised to be calm and reasonable, and not to allow my pride to prevent me from speaking to my brothers and sisters when I returned home.

"When we arrived at the meadow, which was in that part of the 'Plum Trees' known as 'East Swamp,' I asked my father where 'Ivy Island' was.

"'Yonder, at the north end of this meadow, where you see those beautiful trees rising in the distance.'

"All the forenoon I turned grass as fast as two men could cut it, and after a hasty repast at noon, one of our hired men, a good-natured Irishman, named Edmund, took an axe on his shoulder and announced that he was ready to accompany me to 'Ivy Island.' We started, and as we approached the north end of the meadow we found the ground swampy and wet and were soon obliged to leap from bog to bog on our route. A mis-step brought me up to my middle in water, and to add to the dilemma a swarm of hornets attacked me. Attaining the altitude of another bog I was cheered by the assurance that there was only a quarter of a mile of this kind of travel to the edge of my property. I waded on. In about fifteen minutes more, after floundering through the morass, I found myself half-drowned, hornet-stung, mud covered, and out of breath, on comparatively dry land.

"'Never mind, my boy,' said Edmund, 'we have only to cross this little creek, and ye'll be upon your own valuable property.'

"We were on the margin of a stream, the banks of which were thickly covered with alders. I now discovered the use of Edmund's axe, for he felled a small oak to form a temporary bridge to my 'Island' property. Crossing over, I proceeded to the center of my domain. I saw nothing but a few stunted ivies and straggling trees. The truth flashed upon me. I had been the laughing-stock of the family and neighborhood for years. My valuable 'Ivy Island' was an almost inaccessible, worthless bit of barren land, and while I stood deploring my sudden downfall, a huge black snake (one of my tenants) approached me with upraised head. I gave one shriek and rushed for the bridge.

"This was my first and last visit to 'Ivy Island.' My father asked me 'how I liked my property?,' and I responded that I would sell it pretty cheap."

Nonfiction

Cause-Effect Organizer

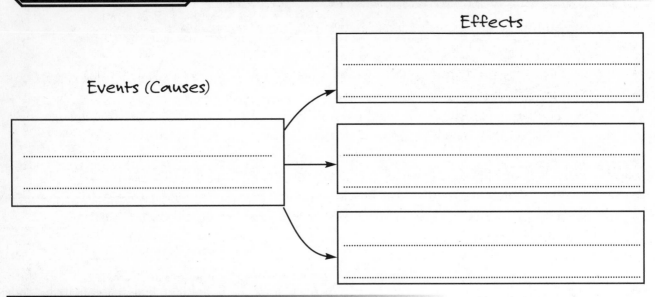

Effects

Events (Causes)

Look for Information

Often you will need to make inferences about how an event affected the subject's life. Use an Inference Chart to organize your thoughts.

Directions: Read the excerpts about Barnum in the chart below. Then note what you can infer about him.

Inference Chart

Text Details	What I've Inferred about Barnum
One night, when he was ten years old, he was called out of bed by his teacher, who had made a wager with a neighbor that Barnum could calculate the number of feet in a load of wood in five minutes. Barnum did it in less than two minutes.	
Before he was five years old he had begun to hoard pennies and "fourpences," and at six years old he was able to exchange his copper bits for a whole silver dollar, the possession of which made him feel richer than he ever felt afterward in all his life.	
"This was my first and last visit to 'Ivy Island.' My father asked me 'how I liked my property?,' and I responded that I would sell it pretty cheap."	

Understanding How Biographies Are Organized

Good biographers include stories that can help the reader form a strong impression of the subject.

- **Think of a biography as a series of stories that offer clues about the subject's personality.**

Directions: What is your impression thus far of P. T. Barnum? Make notes on the following Character Map.

Character Map

How he acts and feels	How others feel about him

P. T. Barnum

How he looks and talks	How I feel about him

E Connect

The personal connections you make when reading a biography can sharpen your impression of the subject.

- **Connect to a biography by asking yourself, "How do I feel about the subject?"**

Directions: Reread this passage from the biography. Then, make your observations on the sticky.

At an early age he manifested a strong development of the good old Yankee organ of acquisitiveness. Before he was five years old he had begun to hoard pennies and "fourpences," and at six years old he was able to exchange his copper bits for a whole silver dollar, the possession of which made him feel richer than he ever felt afterward in all his life. Nor did he lay the dollar away in a napkin, but used it in business to gain more. He would get ten cents a day for riding a horse before the plow, and he would add it to his capital. On holidays other boys spent all their savings, but not so he. Such days were to him opportunities for gain, not for squandering.

P. T. Barnum reminds me of

After Reading

When you finish a biography, think about what you've learned.

F   Pause and Reflect

Ask yourself questions about the biographical subject and your purpose for reading.

- **To reflect on your purpose, ask yourself, "Can I speak knowledgeably about the biographical subject?"**

<u>Directions:</u> Answer these questions about P. T. Barnum.

Questions

Can I name several events in the subject's life?

Do I understand how these events affected the subject?

Do I have a sense of what the person was really like?

Can I say how I feel about the subject?

Can I support how I feel with evidence from the text?

G   Reread

No reader can absorb every detail on a single reading. If you find you don't have a clear impression of the subject, you'll need to do some rereading.

- **The rereading strategy of outlining can help you find and process additional details about the biographical subject.**

Directions: Reread key parts of the excerpt. Then, write details about P. T. Barnum on this Outline.

◄ Outline ▬▬▬▬▬▬▬▬▬▬▬▬▬▬▬▬▬▬▬▬▬▬▬▬▬▬▬▬

P. T. Barnum: Early Years
I. Important event #1: Grandfather bestows "Ivy Island."
A.
B.
II. Important event #2:
A.
B.
III. Important event #3:
A.
B.

H **Remember**

Good readers remember what they've read. Making a map or a sketch can help.

- **Creating a map or sketch can help you retain what you've learned about the subject.**

Directions: Make a sketch of P. T. Barnum on Ivy Island.

◄ Sketch ▬▬▬▬▬▬▬▬▬▬▬▬▬▬▬▬▬▬▬▬▬▬▬▬▬▬▬▬

Nonfiction

Reading a  Memoir

In a memoir, a writer describes some important events from his or her life. The writer reflects on the meaning of those events and their influence.

Before Reading

Here, you'll use the reading process and the strategy of synthesizing to help you read an excerpt from Harriet Jacobs's memoir, *Incidents in the Life of a Slave Girl*.

A Set a Purpose

Your purpose in reading a memoir is twofold. First, you need to understand the life experiences the writer describes. Second, you need to form your own impression of the writer and the people, places, times, and events described.

- **To set your purpose, ask two questions about the writer of the memoir.**

Directions: Ask two questions about Harriet Jacobs or her memoir.

Purpose question #1
....

....

Purpose question #2
....

....

B Preview

After you set your purpose, begin your preview of the memoir. Look carefully at the front and back covers of the book. What information can you find that helps you meet your purpose?

Directions: Preview the front and back covers of *Incidents in the Life of a Slave Girl* on the next page. Make notes on the stickies.

NAME

Nonfiction

Back Cover

Reader, be assured this narrative is no fiction. I am aware that some of my adventures may seem incredible; but they are, nevertheless, strictly true. I have not exaggerated the wrongs inflicted by slavery; on the contrary, my descriptions fall far short of the facts. . . .

I wish I were more competent to the task I have undertaken. But I trust my readers will excuse deficiencies in consideration of circumstances. I was born and reared in slavery; and I remained in a slave state twenty-seven years. Since I have been in the North, it has been necessary for me to work diligently for my own support, and the education of my children. This has not left me much leisure to make up for the loss of early opportunities to improve myself; and it has compelled me to write these pages at irregular intervals, whenever I could snatch an hour from household duties.

Front Cover

INCIDENTS
IN THE
LIFE OF A SLAVE GIRL.
WRITTEN BY HERSELF.

"Northerners know nothing at all about slavery. They think it is perpetual bondage only. They have no conception of the depth of degradation involved in that word, SLAVERY; if they had, they would never cease their efforts until so horrible a system was overthrown."
A WOMAN OF NORTH CAROLINA

Important details I noticed:

detail #1

detail #2

detail #3

The title

The quotes tell me

NAME ....

FOR USE WITH PAGES 210–224

C Plan

When you've finished previewing, make a reading plan that will help you meet your purpose.

> • **Use the strategy of synthesizing to help you get a feel for the "big picture" the writer is presenting.**

Synthesizing is a little like putting together a jigsaw puzzle. When all the pieces are in place, you have a completed picture. In a memoir, the puzzle pieces are the events the writer describes. The big picture is the self-portrait the writer is creating from all the events narrated.

During Reading

D Read with a Purpose

As you read, note the key experiences in the writer's life. Think about how the experiences affected the writer.

Directions: Do a careful reading of the excerpt from Harriet Jacobs's memoir. Make notes on the Key Word or Topic Notes on page 99.

from *Incidents in the Life of a Slave Girl* by Harriet Jacobs

I was born a slave; but I never knew it till six years of happy childhood had passed away. My father was a carpenter, and considered so intelligent and skillful in his trade, that, when buildings out of the common line were to be erected, he was sent for from long distances, to be head workman.

On condition of paying his mistress two hundred dollars a year, and supporting himself, he was allowed to work at his trade, and manage his own affairs. His strongest wish was to purchase his children; but, though he several times offered his hard earnings for that purpose, he never succeeded.

In complexion my parents were a light shade of brownish yellow, and were termed mulattoes. They lived together in a comfortable home; and, though we were all slaves, I was so fondly shielded that I never dreamed I was a piece of merchandise, trusted to them for safe keeping, and liable to be demanded of them at any moment.

I had one brother, William, who was two years younger than myself—a bright, affectionate child. I had also a great treasure in my maternal grandmother, who was a remarkable woman in many respects. She was the daughter of a planter in South Carolina, who, at his death, left her mother and his three children free, with money to go to St. Augustine, where they had relatives. It was during the Revolutionary War; and they were captured on their passage, carried back, and sold to different purchasers.

Such was the story my grandmother used to tell me; but I do not remember all the particulars. She was a little girl when she was captured and sold to the keeper of a

from *Incidents in the Life of a Slave Girl* by Harriet Jacobs

large hotel. I have often heard her tell how hard she fared during childhood. But as she grew older she evinced so much intelligence, and was so faithful, that her master and mistress could not help seeing it was for their interest to take care of such a valuable piece of property.

Stop and Organize

Make some notes about Jacobs on your Key Word or Topic Notes on page 99.

She became an indispensable personage in the household, officiating in all capacities, from cook and wet nurse to seamstress. She was much praised for her cooking; and her nice crackers became so famous in the neighborhood that many people were desirous of obtaining them. In consequence of numerous requests of this kind, she asked permission of her mistress to bake crackers at night, after all the household work was done; and she obtained leave to do it, provided she would clothe herself and her children from the profits.

Upon these terms, after working hard all day for her mistress, she began her midnight bakings, assisted by her two oldest children. The business proved profitable; and each year she laid by a little, which was saved for a fund to purchase her children. Her master died, and the property was divided among his heirs. The widow had her dower in the hotel, which she continued to keep open. My grandmother remained in her service as a slave; but her children were divided among her master's children. As she had five, Benjamin, the youngest one, was sold, in order that each heir might have an equal portion of dollars and cents.

There was so little difference in our ages that he seemed more like my brother than my uncle. He was a bright, handsome lad, nearly white; for he inherited the complexion my grandmother had derived from Anglo-Saxon ancestors. Though only ten years old, seven hundred and twenty dollars were paid for him. His sale was a terrible blow to my grandmother; but she was naturally hopeful, and she went to work with renewed energy, trusting in time to be able to purchase some of her children.

She had laid up three hundred dollars, which her mistress one day begged as a loan, promising to pay her soon. The reader probably knows that no promise or writing given to a slave is legally binding; for, according to Southern laws, a slave, being property, can hold no property. When my grandmother lent her hard earnings to her mistress, she trusted solely to her honor. The honor of a slaveholder to a slave!

Stop and Organize

Make more notes about Jacobs on the Key Word or Topic Notes on page 99.

from *Incidents in the Life of a Slave Girl* by Harriet Jacobs

To this good grandmother I was indebted for many comforts. My brother Willie and I often received portions of the crackers, cakes, and preserves, she made to sell; and after we ceased to be children we were indebted to her for many more important services.

Such were the unusually fortunate circumstances of my early childhood. When I was six years old, my mother died; and then, for the first time, I learned, by the talk around me, that I was a slave.

My mother's mistress was the daughter of my grandmother's mistress. She was the foster sister of my mother; they were both nourished at my grandmother's breast. In fact, my mother had been weaned at three months old, that the babe of the mistress might obtain sufficient food. They played together as children; and, when they became women, my mother was a most faithful servant to her whiter foster sister. On her death-bed her mistress promised that her children should never suffer for any thing; and during her lifetime she kept her word.

They all spoke kindly of my dead mother, who had been a slave merely in name, but in nature was noble and womanly. I grieved for her, and my young mind was troubled with the thought of who would now take care of me and my little brother. I was told that my home was now to be with her mistress; and I found it a happy one. No toilsome or disagreeable duties were imposed upon me. My mistress was so kind to me that I was always glad to do her bidding, and proud to labor for her as much as my young years would permit.

I would sit by her side for hours, sewing diligently, with a heart as free from care as that of any free-born white child. When she thought I was tired, she would send me out to run and jump; and away I bounded, to gather berries or flowers to decorate her room. Those were happy days—too happy to last. The slave child had no thought for the morrow; but there came that blight, which too surely waits on every human being born to be a chattel.

When I was nearly twelve years old, my kind mistress sickened and died. As I saw the cheek grow paler, and the eye more glassy, how earnestly I prayed in my heart that she might live! I loved her; for she had been almost like a mother to me. My prayers were not answered. She died, and they buried her in the little churchyard, where, day after day, my tears fell upon her grave.

Stop and Organize
Make more notes about Jacobs on your Key Word or Topic Notes on page 99.

I was sent to spend a week with my grandmother. I was now old enough to begin to think of the future; and again and again I asked myself what they would do with me. I felt sure I should never find another mistress so kind as the one who was gone. She had promised my dying mother that her children should never suffer for any

NAME ....

from *Incidents in the Life of a Slave Girl* by Harriet Jacobs

thing; and when I remembered that, and recalled her many proofs of attachment to me, I could not help having some hopes that she had left me free. My friends were almost certain it would be so. They thought she would be sure to do it, on account of my mother's love and faithful service. But, alas! we all know that the memory of a faithful slave does not avail much to save her children from the auction block.

After a brief period of suspense, the will of my mistress was read, and we learned that she had bequeathed me to her sister's daughter, a child of five years old. So vanished our hopes. My mistress had taught me the precepts of God's Word: "Thou shalt love thy neighbor as thyself." "Whatsoever ye would that men should do unto you, do ye even so unto them." But I was her slave, and I suppose she did not recognize me as her neighbor.

I would give much to blot out from my memory that one great wrong. As a child, I loved my mistress; and, looking back on the happy days I spent with her, I try to think with less bitterness of this act of injustice. While I was with her, she taught me to read and spell; and for this privilege, which so rarely falls to the lot of a slave, I bless her memory.

She possessed but few slaves; and at her death those were all distributed among her relatives. Five of them were my grandmother's children, and had shared the same milk that nourished her mother's children. Notwithstanding my grandmother's long and faithful service to her owners, not one of her children escaped the auction block. These God-breathing machines are no more, in the sight of their masters, than the cotton they plant, or the horses they tend.

Key Word or Topic Notes

Key Topics	Notes from Reading
period the writer focuses on	
physical surroundings	
work	
major problems	
personality and character	

Using the Strategy

Use the strategy of synthesizing to help you "see" the portrait the writer has created.

Directions: Complete this Web about Harriet Jacobs. Refer to your notes as needed.

◄ Web

Proof:

Proof:

Proof:

Trait:

Trait:

HARRIET JACOBS

Proof:

Trait:

Proof:

Proof:

Understanding How Memoirs Are Organized

Most writers use chronological order to structure their memoirs. This means that they describe the events in the order in which they occurred. Then, they explain their thoughts and feelings about the events.

• **Sequence Notes can help you track the major events in the writer's life.**

Directions: Record four key events from Jacobs's life on this organizer.

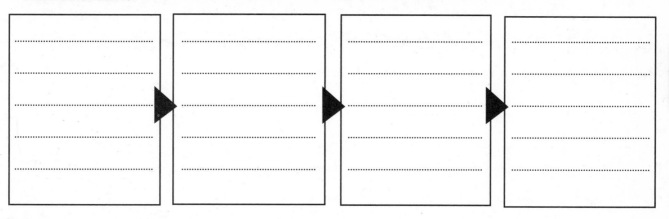

E **Connect**

At this point, think about the second part of your reading purpose: to form an impression of the writer and the people, places, and events she describes.

• **Connect to a memoir by recording your thoughts and feelings about the writer.**

Directions: On the lines below, write your impressions of Harriet Jacobs. Support what you say with "proof" from the excerpt.

....

....

....

....

....

....

....

Nonfiction

After Reading

Take the time now to think about what you've learned.

F Pause and Reflect

At this point, you'll want to return to your reading purpose and think about whether you've accomplished what you set out to do.

- **After you finish a memoir, ask yourself, "How well did I meet my purpose?"**

<u>Directions:</u> Answer these questions about Harriet Jacobs.

Looking Back

Have I been able to form an impression of the writer?

Do I have a clear understanding of the people, places, times, and events the writer describes?

Do I know how I feel about the writer?

Do I understand the purpose of the memoir?

G Reread

If you feel you haven't met your purpose, spend a few minutes rereading. Choose a rereading strategy that will help you locate the information you need.

- **A powerful rereading strategy to use with a memoir is visualizing and thinking aloud.**

When you visualize, you make mental pictures of what you are reading. When you think aloud, you talk to yourself about what you've learned.

Directions: Make a quick sketch of the "midnight baking" Jacobs describes. Show both Harriet and her grandmother in the sketch. Then, write a Think Aloud that explains what they're doing and why they're doing it.

◄ **Visualizing**

H Remember

If you've read a memoir for a class assignment, you need to find a way to remember the most important details and your impression of the writer.

• **Writing a book review can help you retain what you've learned.**

Directions: Write a review of this chapter from *Incidents in the Life of a Slave Girl*. Open with your impression of Harriet Jacobs. Then, explain why you would or would not like to read more of her story.

◄ **Book Review**

Incidents in the Life of a Slave Girl

NAME ....

FOR USE WITH PAGES 225–234

Focus on Persuasive Writing

Persuasive writing makes an argument or attempts to prove something is true. Your job is to understand and evaluate the argument the writer presents. A three-step plan will help.

Step 1 Find the topic.

As a first step, find the topic. Ask yourself, "What is the writer mostly talking about?"

Directions: Read this editorial. Make notes on the stickies.

Cell Phone and Beeper Ban for the Birds

Yesterday morning, Principal Jameel Roberts announced a school-wide ban on pagers and cell phones. The ban will go into effect Monday of next week. Beginning that day, teachers are required to confiscate any cell phone or pager they see and turn it over to the principal's office. Repeat offenders will be suspended.

Principal Roberts says that this "digital ban" is in the students' best interest. He told an assembly of 10th, 11th, and 12th grade students that he is instituting the ban because cell phones and pagers are disruptive and distracting. He also expressed concern that in some schools, students use these digital devices to conduct illegal activities.

But is it fair for Principal Roberts to punish students at our school for the misdeeds of students at other schools? Here at Emerson High, there is no evidence that students are using cell phones and pagers for illegal activities. In fact, most students use their cell phones and pagers for *admirable* activities like setting up study groups, consulting with each other about missed assignments, and so on.

Furthermore, there is no evidence that cell phones or pagers are disruptive. As a courtesy, most students turn their electronics off or activate a "silent ring" feature when they are in class. They don't sit and talk on the phone in the middle of the class or send pages to friends while the teacher is lecturing. It just doesn't happen.

As a final point, I wonder how the digital ban will affect the staff of

⬦ "Cell Phone and Beeper Ban for the Birds" ⬦

Emerson High. How many teachers carry cell phones or pagers with them in their pockets or purses? It's a safe bet that most of them do. Teachers need these devices for the same reason students do: to keep in touch.

So it would seem that Principal Roberts needs to reconsider his digital ban. Students need cell phones, teachers need cell phones, and even school principals need cell phones. What's the point of fighting it?

The title/headline is:
....
....
....

The topic is
....
....
....

Step 2 Find the assertion and support.

The assertion is a statement of belief that the writer explains and supports.

Directions: Reread the editorial. Write the author's assertion on the lines below.

The writer's assertion is
....

....

Step 3 Evaluate the argument.

As a final step, decide how you feel about the argument.

Directions: Complete this Argument Chart. Write the viewpoint and evidence. Then evaluate the argument.

◄ Argument Chart

Assertion	Support	My Opinion

NAME ....

FOR USE WITH PAGES 235–245

Focus on Speeches

When you read a speech, try to imagine how the speaker sounds. Then, use the reading process to understand and evaluate the speaker's message.

Step 1 Learn about the speaker and purpose of the speech.

Your first step will be to find out what you can about the speaker and the purpose of the speech.

Directions: Read this speech. Make notes on the Web that follows.

"Let Me Be a Free Man" by Chief Joseph, Nez Percé Nation

Chief Joseph (1840–1904) of the Nez Percé Nation is remembered for his dramatic effort to move members of his tribe to Canada after the news that whites would be permitted to settle the Oregon Territory. In 1877, Chief Joseph and his followers were captured and forced onto a barren reservation in Oklahoma. In the speech that follows, he begs for the right for his people to remain free.

If the white man wants to live in peace with the Indian, he can live in peace. . . . Treat all men alike. Give them all the same law. Give them all an even chance to live and grow. All men were made by the same Great Spirit Chief. They are all brothers. The Earth is the mother of all people, and all people should have equal rights upon it. . . .Let me be a free man, free to travel, free to stop, free to work, free to trade . . . where I choose my own teachers, free to follow the religion of my fathers, free to think and talk and act for myself, and I will obey every law, or submit to the penalty.

Web

When

Where

"Chief Joseph's speech"

Why

Step 2 Understand the organization.

Not every line in a speech is equally important. Look for key lines and mark them. They can help you figure out the speaker's message.

Directions: Reread Chief Joseph's speech. Highlight the most important lines.

Step 3 Find the viewpoint.

The speaker's opinion or main idea is called the "viewpoint." Use this formula to find the viewpoint:

Subject of the Speech + Speaker's Opinion of the Subject = The Speaker's Main Idea or Viewpoint

Directions: Use the formula to find the viewpoint of Chief Joseph's speech.

Subject of the Speech + Speaker's Opinion of the Subject = The Speaker's Main Idea or Viewpoint

....

....

....

....

....

....

Step 4 Locate support for the viewpoint.

A good speaker will support his or her viewpoint with plenty of details.

Directions: Make notes about Chief Joseph's viewpoint and support on this Evidence Organizer.

Evidence Organizer

Viewpoint:			
Detail 1	**Detail 2**	**Detail 3**	**Detail 4**

Reading a  Short Story

Reading a short story can be one of life's greatest pleasures. But there is no pleasure without comprehension. The reading process can help you understand what you're reading.

Before Reading

Let the reading process and the strategy of synthesizing help you read and respond to the short story "The Last Leaf" by O. Henry.

A Set a Purpose

Beginning by setting your purpose will help you get more from the short story you're about to read.

• **To set your purpose, ask important questions about the major elements of the story.**

<u>Directions:</u> Write your purpose questions in the second column.

Purpose Chart

Element	My Questions
characters	
setting	
plot	
dialogue	
point of view	

Fiction

B Preview

You read better if you know what to expect. A preview can clue you in as to what's to come.

Directions: Preview "The Last Leaf." Answer the questions that follow. Then, make a prediction about the story.

Preview Chart

Who is the author of the story?

What did you find out about the point of view?

What did you learn from the first few paragraphs?

What repeated words did you notice?

My prediction:

"The Last Leaf" by O. Henry

What you need to know . . .

THE SELECTION In "The Last Leaf," a young woman struggles to help her friend recover from a deadly case of pneumonia.

THE AUTHOR O. Henry was the pen name for William Sidney Porter (1862–1910). He was one of the best short story writers in American history. His love for ordinary men and women who live ordinary lives resonates in the great majority of his stories. "The Last Leaf" is one of his most sentimental—and popular—stories.

THE THEME determination

LITERARY FOCUS characterization

FURTHER READING "The Gift of the Magi" and "The Ransom of Red Chief"

In a little district west of Washington Square the streets have run crazy and broken themselves into small strips called "places." These "places" make strange angles and curves. One street crosses itself a time or two. An artist once discovered a valuable possibility in this street. Suppose a collector with a bill for paints, paper, and canvas should, in traversing this route, suddenly meet himself coming back, without a cent having been paid on account!

So, to quaint old Greenwich Village the art people soon came prowling, hunting for north windows and eighteenth-century gables and Dutch attics and low rents. Then they imported some pewter mugs and a chafing dish or two from Sixth Avenue, and became a "colony."

Fiction

111

"The Last Leaf" by O. Henry

At the top of a squatty, three-story brick house Sue and Johnsy had their studio. "Johnsy" was familiar for Joanna. One was from Maine; the other from California. They had met at the *table d'hôte* of an Eighth street "Delmonico's" and found their tastes in art and chicory salad so congenial that the joint studio resulted.

That was in May. In November a cold, unseen stranger, whom the doctors called Pneumonia, stalked about the colony, touching one here and there with his icy finger. Over on the east side this ravager strode boldly, smiting his victims by scores, but his feet trod slowly through the maze of the narrow and moss-grown "places."

Stop and Organize
Make some notes in the "Setting" section of the Synthesizing Chart on page 116.

Mr. Pneumonia was not what you would call a chivalric old gentleman. A mite of a little woman with blood thinned by California zephyrs was hardly fair game for the red-fisted, short-breathed old duffer. But Johnsy he smote; and she lay, scarcely moving, on her painted iron bedstead, looking through the small Dutch windowpanes at the blank side of the next brick house.

One morning the busy doctor invited Sue into the hallway with a shaggy, grey eyebrow.

"She has one chance in, let us say, ten," he said, as he shook down the mercury in his clinical thermometer. "And that chance is for her to want to live. This way people have of lining-up on the side of the undertaker makes the entire pharmacopoeia[1] look silly. Your little lady has made up her mind that she's not going to get well. Has she anything on her mind?"

"She wanted to paint the Bay of Naples some day," said Sue.

"Paint? Bosh! Has she anything on her mind worth thinking about twice—a man, for instance?"

"A man?" said Sue, with a twang in her voice. "Is a man worth—but no, doctor; there is nothing of the kind."

"Well, it is the weakness, then," said the doctor. "I will do all that science, so far as it may filter through my efforts, can accomplish. But whenever my patient begins to count the carriages in her funeral procession I subtract 50 percent from the curative power of medicines. If you will get her to ask one question about the new winter styles in cloak sleeves I will promise you a one-in-five chance for her, instead of one in ten."

1. **pharmacopoeia**—the book of drugs and pharmaceuticals a doctor might prescribe.

NAME ....

After the doctor had gone, Sue went into the workroom and cried a Japanese napkin to a pulp. Then she swaggered into Johnsy's room with her drawing-board, whistling ragtime.

Johnsy lay, scarcely making a ripple under the bedclothes, with her face toward the window. Sue stopped whistling, thinking she was asleep.

She arranged her board and began a pen-and-ink drawing to illustrate a magazine story. Young artists must pave their way to Art by drawing pictures for magazine stories that young authors write to pave their way to Literature.

As Sue was sketching a pair of elegant horse show riding trousers and a monocle on the figure of the hero, an Idaho cowboy, she heard a low sound, several times repeated. She went quickly to the bedside.

Johnsy's eyes were open wide. She was looking out the window and counting backward.

"Twelve," she said, and a little later, "eleven"; and then "ten," and "nine"; and then "eight" and "seven," almost together.

Sue looked solicitously out the window. What was there to count? There was only a bare, dreary yard to be seen, and the blank side of the brick house twenty feet away. An old, old ivy vine, gnarled and decayed at the roots, climbed half-way up the brick wall. The cold breath of autumn had stricken its leaves from the vine until its skeleton branches clung, almost bare, to the crumbling bricks.

"What is it, dear?" asked Sue.

"Six," said Johnsy, in almost a whisper. "They're falling faster now. Three days ago there were almost a hundred. It made my head ache to count them. But now it's easy. There goes another one. There are only five left now."

"Five what, dear? Tell your Sudie."

"Leaves. On the ivy vine. When the last one falls I must go too. I've known that for three days. Didn't the doctor tell you?"

"Oh, I never heard of such nonsense!" complained Sue, with magnificent scorn. "What have old ivy leaves to do with your getting well? And you used to love that vine so, you naughty girl. Don't be a goosey. Why, the doctor told me this morning that your chances for getting well real soon were let's see exactly what he said—he said the chances were ten to one! Why, that's almost as good a chance as we have in New York when we ride on the street cars or walk past a new building. Try to take some broth now, and let Sudie go back to her drawing, so she can sell the editor man with it, and buy port wine for her sick child, and pork chops for her greedy self."

"You needn't get any more wine," said Johnsy, keeping her eyes fixed out the window. "There goes another. No, I don't want any broth. That leaves just four. I want to see the last one fall before it gets dark. Then I'll go too."

"Johnsy, dear," said Sue, bending over her, "will you promise me to keep your eyes closed, and not look out the window until I am done working? I must hand these drawings in by to-morrow. I need the light, or I would draw the shade down."

NAME ....

FOR USE WITH PAGES 267–287

"The Last Leaf" by O. Henry

"Couldn't you draw in the other room?" asked Johnsy coldly.

"I'd rather be here by you," said Sue. "Besides, I don't want you to keep looking at those silly ivy leaves."

"Tell me as soon as you have finished," said Johnsy, closing her eyes, and lying white and still as a fallen statue, "because I want to see the last one fall. I'm tired of waiting. I'm tired of thinking. I want to turn loose my hold on everything, and go sailing down, down, just like one of those poor, tired leaves."

"Try to sleep," said Sue. "I must call Behrman up to be my model for the old hermit miner. I'll not be gone a minute. Don't try to move till I come back."

Old Behrman was a painter who lived on the ground floor beneath them. He was past sixty and had a Michelangelo's Moses beard curling down from the head of a satyr along the body of an imp. Behrman was a failure in art. Forty years he had wielded the brush without getting near enough to touch the hem of his Mistress's robe. He had been always about to paint a masterpiece, but had never yet begun it. For several years he had painted nothing except now and then a daub in the line of commerce or advertising. He earned a little by serving as a model to those young artists in the colony who could not pay the price of a professional. He drank gin to excess, and still talked of his coming masterpiece. For the rest he was a fierce little old man, who scoffed terribly at softness in any one, and who regarded himself as especial mastiff-in-waiting to protect the two young artists in the studio above.

Sue found Behrman smelling strongly of juniper berries[2] in his dimly lighted den below. In one corner was a blank canvas on an easel that had been waiting there for twenty-five years to receive the first line of the masterpiece. She told him of Johnsy's fancy, and how she feared she would, indeed, light and fragile as a leaf herself, float away when her slight hold upon the world grew weaker.

Old Behrman, with his red eyes plainly streaming, shouted his contempt and derision for such idiotic imaginings.

"Vass!" he cried. "Is dere people in de world mit der foolishness to die because leafs dey drop off from a confounded vine? I haf not heard of such a thing. No, I vill not bose as a model for your fool hermit-dunderhead. Vy do you allow dot silly business to come in der brain of her? Ach, dot poor lettle Miss Yohnsy."

"She is very ill and weak," said Sue, "and the fever has left her mind morbid and full of strange fancies. Very well, Mr. Behrman, if you do not care to pose for me, you needn't. But I think you are a horrid old—old flibbertigibbet."

"You are just like a woman!" yelled Behrman. "Who said I vill not bose? Go on. I come mit you. For half an hour I haf peen trying to say dot I am ready to bose. Gott! Dis is not any blace in which one so goot as Miss Yohnsy shall lie sick. Some day I vill baint a masterpiece, and ve shall all go avay. Gott! yes."

2. juniper berries—i.e., smelling of gin.

"The Last Leaf" by O. Henry

Stop and Organize

Make some notes in the "Characters" and "Dialogue" sections of the Synthesizing Chart on page 117.

Johnsy was sleeping when they went upstairs. Sue pulled the shade down to the window-sill, and motioned Behrman into the other room. In there they peered out the window fearfully at the ivy vine. Then they looked at each other for a moment without speaking. A persistent, cold rain was falling, mingled with snow. Behrman, in his old blue shirt, took his seat as the hermit-miner on an upturned kettle for a rock.

When Sue awoke from an hour's sleep the next morning she found Johnsy, with dull, wide-open eyes staring at the drawn green shade.

"Pull it up; I want to see," she ordered in a whisper.

Wearily Sue obeyed. But lo! after the beating rain and fierce gusts of wind that had endured through the livelong night, there yet stood out against the brick wall one ivy leaf. It was the last on the vine. Still dark-green near its stem, but with its serrated edges tinted with the yellow of dissolution and decay, it hung bravely from a branch some twenty feet above the ground.

"It is the last one," said Johnsy. "I thought it would surely fall during the night. I heard the wind. It will fall to-day, and I shall die at the same time."

"Dear, dear!" said Sue, leaning her worn face down to the pillow; "think of me, if you won't think of yourself. What would I do?"

But Johnsy did not answer. The lonesomest thing in all the world is a soul when it is making ready to go on its mysterious, far journey. The fancy seemed to possess her more strongly as one by one the ties that bound her to friendship and to earth were loosed.

The day wore away, and even through the twilight they could see the lone ivy leaf clinging to its stem against the wall. And then, with the coming of the night the north wind was again loosed, while the rain still beat against the windows and pattered down from the low Dutch eaves.

When it was light enough Johnsy, the merciless, commanded that the shade be raised.

The ivy leaf was still there.

Johnsy lay for a long time looking at it. And then she called to Sue, who was stirring her chicken broth over the gas stove.

"I've been a bad girl, Sudie," said Johnsy. "Something has made that last leaf stay there to show me how wicked I was. It is a sin to want to die. You may bring me a little broth now, and some milk with a little port in it, and no; bring me a hand-mirror first; and then pack some pillows about me, and I will sit up and watch you cook."

An hour later she said "Sudie, some day I hope to paint the Bay of Naples."

Fiction

"The Last Leaf" by O. Henry

The doctor came in the afternoon, and Sue had an excuse to go into the hallway as he left.

"Even chances," said the doctor, taking Sue's thin, shaking hand in his. "With good nursing you'll win. And now I must see another case I have downstairs. Behrman, he is some kind of an artist, I believe. Pneumonia, too. He is an old, weak man, and the attack is acute. There is no hope for him; but he goes to the hospital to-day to be made more comfortable."

The next day the doctor said to Sue: "She's out of danger. You've won. Nutrition and care now that's all."

And that afternoon Sue came to the bed where Johnsy lay contentedly knitting a very blue and very useless woolen shoulder scarf, and put one arm around her, pillows and all.

"I have something to tell you, white mouse," she said. "Mr. Behrman died of pneumonia to-day in the hospital. He was ill only two days. The janitor found him on the morning of the first day in his room downstairs helpless with pain. His shoes and clothing were wet through and icy cold. They couldn't imagine where he had been on such a dreadful night. And then they found a lantern, still lighted, and a ladder that had been dragged from its place and some scattered brushes, and a palette with green and yellow colors mixed on it, and look out the window, dear, at the last ivy leaf on the wall. Didn't you wonder why it never fluttered or moved when the wind blew? Ah, darling, it's Behrman's masterpiece—he painted it there the night that the last leaf fell."

Stop and Organize

Make some notes in the "Plot" section of the Synthesizing Chart on page 117.

Plan

Next, choose a strategy that can help you meet your purpose.

• Practice the strategy of synthesizing.

When you synthesize, you look at a number of elements and pull them together to form a new product.

During Reading

 Read with a Purpose

Directions: Do a careful reading of "The Last Leaf." Write your notes on this organizer. If you need help, see pages 277–279 of the *Reader's Handbook*.

Synthesizing Chart

Write facts from the story here.	Write your thoughts or the most important thoughts here.
Characters	
Setting	
Plot	
Dialogue	
Theme	

Fiction

Using the Strategy

There are many different types of reading tools that can help you synthesize the elements in a story.

• A Story Organizer will help you reflect on the plot of a story.

Directions: Make notes about the plot and theme of "The Last Leaf" on the Story Organizer below.

Story Organizer

Beginning	Middle	End

Possible Theme:

Understanding How Short Stories Are Organized

A short story's plot can be divided into five basic parts: exposition, rising action, climax, falling action, and resolution.

Directions: Use the Plot Diagram on the next page to show the organization of "The Last Leaf." See page 280 of the *Reader's Handbook* if you need help.

NAME ....

FOR USE WITH PAGES 267–287

Plot Diagram

Climax

On the lines, write
what happens in each
part of the story.

Rising Action

Falling Action

Exposition

Resolution

Connect

You'll remember and enjoy a short story better if you connect it to your
own life.

• **Use a Making Connections Chart to think through your feelings about
a story.**

Directions: Complete this chart for "The Last Leaf."

Making Connections Chart

I wonder why . . .	
I think . . .	
This is similar to . . .	
This reminds me of . . .	

After Reading

F Pause and Reflect

It is important when you finish a short story to reflect on the meaning. A good first step is to think about the ending.

- **After you finish a story, ask yourself, "Did things turn out the way I expected?"**

Directions: Answer these questions about "The Last Leaf."

How did you feel when you read the ending of "The Last Leaf"?

Why did you feel this way?

Reread

When you reread, you notice things you missed the first time around. This will sharpen your understanding of the story.

• **A good rereading strategy to use with short stories is close reading.**

<u>Directions:</u> Read the quotations at the left of the organizer below. Skim the story to find where the quote appears. Then respond to each quote.

◄ Close Reading Organizer ►

Text from "The Last Leaf"	What I Think about It
"Paint? Bosh! Has she anything on her mind worth thinking about twice—a man, for instance?"	
"Johnsy, dear," said Sue, bending over her, "will you promise me to keep your eyes closed, and not look out the window until I am done working?"	
For the rest he was a fierce little old man, who scoffed terribly at softness in any one, and who regarded himself as especial mastiff-in-waiting to protect the two young artists in the studio above.	
Behrman was a failure in art.	
"Ah, darling, it's Behrman's masterpiece—he painted it there the night that the last leaf fell."	

Fiction

Remember

Sharing a story can help you remember it. It can also sharpen your comprehension of the most important ideas.

• **To help you remember a story, discuss key aspects of the plot, characters, and theme.**

Directions: Get together in a small group to discuss "The Last Leaf." Use the prompts below, as well as one of your own that you've written beforehand, to stimulate a discussion of the short story. Write your discussion notes on the lines.

Discussion Prompts

What inferences can you make about Johnsy? about Sue? about Behrman?	**How is the leaf Behrman's masterpiece?**

Which character do you think was the most responsible for Johnsy's recovery? Why?	**How would the story be different if it were told from Behrman's point of view?**

My discussion question:

Reading a Novel

Reading a novel is like taking a long and mysterious journey. The reading process is a road map you can use to keep from getting lost. It will can also help you understand and enjoy the people, places, and things you see along the way.

Before Reading

Here, you'll practice using the reading process with an excerpt from the novel *Great Expectations* by Charles Dickens.

A Set a Purpose

Your primary purpose for reading a novel is enjoyment. But if you're reading the book for school, it will be important to recognize and remember the novel's point of view, characters, setting, plot, and theme.

- **To set your purpose, ask important questions about the major literary elements of the novel.**

Directions: You will be reading Chapter 1 of *Great Expectations*. Write your purpose questions on the chart below. (The first one is done for you.)

Purpose Chart

Element	My Questions
point of view	From whose perspective is the story told?
characters	
setting	
plot	
theme	

Fiction

123

B Preview

Always spend a moment or two previewing the novel you're about to read. Begin by examining the front and back covers of the book.

Directions: Preview the front and back covers of *Great Expectations*. Write important facts and details on the sticky notes.

Back Cover

Within these pages find Charles Dickens's tale of Pip's coming of age— one of the most widely read novels of all time.

First published in 1861, *Great Expectations* is the story of a young orphan who travels the gloomy graveyards, damp marshlands, and bustling city streets of Victorian England in search of home and happiness. Along the way, he meets a half-mad spinster, a vicious young woman whose beauty is a weapon, and an escaped convict who carries with him a secret that threatens to bring heartbreak and ruin to everyone Pip has ever known.

Front Cover

GREAT EXPECTATIONS

by Charles Dickens

Important information about the book: _____
_____
_____
_____
_____

Details that relate to my purpose: _____
_____
_____
_____
_____

The title: _____
_____

The author: _____
_____

Plan

After your preview, choose a strategy that can help you respond to the novel.

• **Good readers know that using graphic organizers can help them get more from a novel.**

Directions: Look over the Fiction Organizer so that you will know ahead of time what to pay attention to as you read Chapter 1 of *Great Expectations*.

◄ **Fiction Organizer**

Point of View
....
....
....
....

Characters
....
....
....
....

Charles Dickens, Great Expectations

Setting
....
....
....
....
....
....
....
....

Plot
....
....
....
....
....
....

Theme
....
....
....
....
....
....
....

Fiction

During Reading

D Read with a Purpose

Completing a Fiction Organizer as you read can make it easier to stay focused on your purpose.

Directions: Now, do a careful reading of Chapter 1 of *Great Expectations*. As you read, think about point of view, the characters, setting, plot, and theme.

> ### from *Great Expectations* by Charles Dickens

My father's family name being Pirrip, and my Christian name Philip, my infant tongue could make of both names nothing longer or more explicit than Pip. So, I called myself Pip, and came to be called Pip.

I give Pirrip as my father's family name, on the authority of his tombstone and my sister—Mrs. Joe Gargery, who married the blacksmith. As I never saw my father or my mother, and never saw any likeness of either of them (for their days were long before the days of photographs), my first fancies regarding what they were like, were unreasonably derived from their tombstones. The shape of the letters on my father's, gave me an odd idea that he was a square, stout, dark man, with curly black hair. From the character and turn of the inscription, *"Also Georgiana Wife of the Above,"* I drew a childish conclusion that my mother was freckled and sickly. To five little stone lozenges, each about a foot and a half long, which were arranged in a neat row beside their grave, and were sacred to the memory of five little brothers of mine—who gave up trying to get a living exceedingly early in that universal struggle—I am indebted for a belief I religiously entertained that they had all been born on their backs with their hands in their trousers-pockets, and had never taken them out in this state of existence.

Ours was the marsh country, down by the river, within, as the river wound, twenty miles of the sea. My first most vivid and broad impression of the identity of things, seems to me to have been gained on a memorable raw afternoon towards evening. At such a time I found out for certain, that this bleak place overgrown with nettles was the churchyard; and that Philip Pirrip, late of this parish, and also Georgiana wife of the above, were dead and buried; and that Alexander, Bartholomew, Abraham, Tobias, and Roger, infant children of the aforesaid, were also dead and buried; and that the dark flat wilderness beyond the churchyard, intersected with dykes and mounds and gates, with scattered cattle feeding on it, was the marshes; and that the low leaden line beyond, was the river; and that the distant savage lair from which the wind was rushing, was the sea; and that the small bundle of shivers growing afraid of it all and beginning to cry, was Pip.

Stop and Organize

What is the story's setting? From whose point of view is the story told? Make notes on the Fiction Organizer on page 125.

from *Great Expectations* by Charles Dickens

"Hold your noise!" cried a terrible voice, as a man started up from among the graves at the side of the church porch. "Keep still, you little devil, or I'll cut your throat!"

A fearful man, all in coarse grey, with a great iron on his leg. A man with no hat, and with broken shoes, and with an old rag tied round his head. A man who had been soaked in water, and smothered in mud, and lamed by stones, and cut by flints, and stung by nettles, and torn by briars; who limped, and shivered, and glared and growled; and whose teeth chattered in his head as he seized me by the chin.

"O! Don't cut my throat, sir," I pleaded in terror. "Pray don't do it, sir."

"Tell us your name!" said the man. "Quick!"

"Pip, sir."

"Once more," said the man, staring at me. "Give it mouth!"

"Pip. Pip, sir."

"Show us where you live," said the man. "Pint out the place!"

I pointed to where our village lay, on the flat in-shore among the alder-trees and pollards, a mile or more from the church.

The man, after looking at me for a moment, turned me upside down, and emptied my pockets. There was nothing in them but a piece of bread. When the church came to itself—for he was so sudden and strong that he made it go head over heels before me, and I saw the steeple under my feet—when the church came to itself, I say, I was seated on a high tombstone, trembling, while he ate the bread ravenously.

"You young dog," said the man, licking his lips, "what fat cheeks you ha' got."

I believe they were fat, though I was at that time undersized for my years, and not strong.

"Darn me if I couldn't eat em," said the man, with a threatening shake of his head, "and if I han't half a mind to't!"

I earnestly expressed my hope that he wouldn't, and held tighter to the tombstone on which he had put me; partly, to keep myself upon it; partly, to keep myself from crying.

"Now lookee here!" said the man. "Where's your mother?"

"There, sir!" said I.

He started, made a short run, and stopped and looked over his shoulder.

"There, sir!" I timidly explained. "Also Georgiana. That's my mother."

"Oh!" said he, coming back. "And is that your father alonger your mother?"

"Yes, sir," said I; "him too; late of this parish."

"Ha!" he muttered then, considering. "Who d'ye live with—supposin' you're kindly let to live, which I han't made up my mind about?"

"My sister, sir—Mrs. Joe Gargery—wife of Joe Gargery, the blacksmith, sir."

"Blacksmith, eh?" said he. And looked down at his leg.

After darkly looking at his leg and me several times, he came closer to my tombstone, took me by both arms, and tilted me back as far as he could hold me; so that his eyes looked most powerfully down into mine, and mine looked most helplessly up into his.

NAME ....

FOR USE WITH PAGES 288–312

from *Great Expectations* by Charles Dickens

"Now lookee here," he said, "the question being whether you're to be let to live. You know what a file is?"

"Yes, sir."

"And you know what wittles is?"

"Yes, sir."

After each question he tilted me over a little more, so as to give me a greater sense of helplessness and danger.

"You get me a file." He tilted me again. "And you get me wittles." He tilted me again. "You bring 'em both to me." He tilted me again. "Or I'll have your heart and liver out." He tilted me again.

Stop and Organize

What inferences can you make about Pip? What inferences can you make about the stranger?
Make notes on the Fiction Organizer on page 125.

I was dreadfully frightened, and so giddy that I clung to him with both hands, and said, "If you would kindly please to let me keep upright, sir, perhaps I shouldn't be sick, and perhaps I could attend more."

He gave me a most tremendous dip and roll, so that the church jumped over its own weather-cock. Then, he held me by the arms, in an upright position on the top of the stone, and went on in these fearful terms:

"You bring me, to-morrow morning early, that file and them wittles. You bring the lot to me, at that old Battery over yonder. You do it, and you never dare to say a word or dare to make a sign concerning your having seen such a person as me, or any person sumever, and you shall be let to live. You fail, or you go from my words in any partickler, no matter how small it is, and your heart and your liver shall be tore out, roasted and ate. Now, I ain't alone, as you may think I am. There's a young man hid with me, in comparison with which young man I am a Angel. That young man hears the words I speak. That young man has a secret way pecooliar to himself, of getting at a boy, and at his heart, and at his liver. It is in wain for a boy to attempt to hide himself from that young man. A boy may lock his door, may be warm in bed, may tuck himself up, may draw the clothes over his head, may think himself comfortable and safe, but that young man will softly creep and creep his way to him and tear him open. I am a-keeping that young man from harming of you at the present moment, with great difficulty. I find it wery hard to hold that young man off of your inside. Now, what do you say?"

Stop and Organize

What would you say are some of the big ideas or possible themes in this novel?
Make notes on the Fiction Organizer on page 125.

NAME ....

from *Great Expectations* by Charles Dickens

I said that I would get him the file, and I would get him what broken bits of food I could, and I would come to him at the Battery, early in the morning.

"Say, Lord strike you dead if you don't!" said the man.

I said so, and he took me down.

"Now," he pursued, "you remember what you've undertook, and you remember that young man, and you get home!"

"Goo-good night, sir," I faltered.

"Much of that!" said he, glancing about him over the cold wet flat. "I wish I was a frog. Or a eel!"

At the same time, he hugged his shuddering body in both his arms—clasping himself, as if to hold himself together—and limped towards the low church wall. As I saw him go, picking his way among the nettles, and among the brambles that bound the green mounds, he looked in my young eyes as if he were eluding the hands of the dead people, stretching up cautiously out of their graves, to get a twist upon his ankle and pull him in.

When he came to the low church wall, he got over it, like a man whose legs were numbed and stiff, and then turned round to look for me. When I saw him turning, I set my face towards home, and made the best use of my legs. But presently I looked over my shoulder, and saw him going on again towards the river, still hugging himself in both arms, and picking his way with his sore feet among the great stones dropped into the marshes here and there, for stepping-places when the rains were heavy, or the tide was in.

The marshes were just a long black horizontal line then, as I stopped to look after him; and the river was just another horizontal line, not nearly so broad nor yet so black; and the sky was just a row of long angry red lines and dense black lines intermixed. On the edge of the river I could faintly make out the only two black things in all the prospect that seemed to be standing upright; one of these was the beacon by which the sailors steered—like an unhooped cask upon a pole—an ugly thing when you were near it; the other a gibbet, with some chains hanging to it which had once held a pirate. The man was limping on towards this latter, as if he were the pirate come to life, and come down, and going back to hook himself up again. It gave me a terrible turn when I thought so; and as I saw the cattle lifting their heads to gaze after him, I wondered whether they thought so too. I looked all round for the horrible young man, and could see no signs of him. But, now I was frightened again, and ran home without stopping.

Stop and Organize

What happens in this chapter of the book? What are the key events? Make notes on the Fiction Organizer on page 125.

Using the Strategy

There are all kinds of graphic organizers that you can use with a novel. A Character Map is a good one to use at the beginning of a novel to help you get to know the book's main character.

Directions: Make notes about Pip on this Character Map.

Character Map

How he looks:

How he acts, what he says:

What he thinks, feels:

Pip

How others react to him:

What I've learned about him so far:

Understanding How Novels Are Organized

The plots of most novels are in chronological order. A graphic organizer will help you keep track of what is happening.

• **A Story String can help you see how one event leads to another.**

Directions: Think about what happens in Chapter 1 of *Great Expectations*. Then, make notes on this Story String.

Story String

130

Connect

You can't help but react to the characters and events in a novel. Keeping track of your reactions will help you make sense of a novel.

• **Making connections with a novel means recording your thoughts and feelings about the text.**

Directions: Read the quotes from *Great Expectations* on the left of the Double-entry Journal below. Write how they make you feel or what they remind you of on the right.

Double-Entry Journal

Quotes	My Reactions
A man who had been soaked in water, and smothered in mud, and lamed by stones, and cut by flints, and stung by nettles, and torn by briars; who limped, and shivered, and glared and growled; and whose teeth chattered in his head as he seized me by the chin.	
I was dreadfully frightened, and so giddy that I clung to him with both hands, and said, "If you would kindly please to let me keep upright, sir, perhaps I shouldn't be sick, and perhaps I could attend more."	

After Reading

When you finish reading, it is important to take a moment or two to think about your purpose.

 Pause and Reflect

Keep in mind that your purpose was to find details about point of view, the characters, setting, plot, and theme.

• **After you finish a novel, ask yourself, "How well did I meet my purpose?"**

Fiction

Directions: Answer these questions about the chapter you just read from *Great Expectations*.

Looking Back

Question	My Answer	What I Need to Understand Better
Do I know the point of view?	yes no	
Do I have a strong understanding of the characters I've met thus far?	yes no	
Can I visualize the setting?	yes no	
Do I understand the plot up to this point?	yes no	
Have I begun to think about the big ideas or themes in the work?	yes no	

 Reread

If you haven't met your purpose, you may need to do some rereading. Rather than reread word-for-word, however, you'll want to skim chunks of the novel for clues about one of the major literary elements. The rereading strategy of synthesizing can help.

• **Use synthesizing to help you see how the parts of a novel fit together.**

FOR USE WITH PAGES 288–312

Directions: Complete this synthesizing chart for Chapter 1 of *Great Expectations*. If you need help, see page 279 of the *Reader's Handbook*.

Synthesizing Chart

Great Expectations, Chapter 1	What I Think
Characters	
Setting	
Plot	
Theme	

Fiction

H   Remember

It's important to remember what happens from one chapter to another in a novel.

- **Writing a brief summary of each chapter will help you keep track of what happens in a novel.**

Directions: Write a brief summary of Chapter 1 of *Great Expectations*.

Summary

Great Expectations

Chapter 1

Focus on

Plot is the arrangement of events in a work of fiction. In this lesson, you'll explore the plot of a Greek myth.

Step 1 Track the key events.

On your first reading of a story, keep an eye on what happens in the plot.

Directions: Read this myth about Pandora. Underline key events in the plot. Make any notes on the stickies.

"Pandora" by Edith Hamilton

Another story about Pandora is that the source of all misfortune was not her wicked nature, but only her curiosity. The gods presented her with a box into which each had put something harmful, and forbade her to ever open it. Then they sent her to Epimetheus, who took her gladly although Prometheus had warned him never to accept anything from Zeus. He took her, and afterward when that dangerous thing, a woman, was his, he understood how good his brother's advice had been. For Pandora *had* to know what was in the box. One day she lifted the lid—and out flew plagues innumerable, sorrow, and mischief for mankind. In terror Pandora clapped the lid down, but too late. One good thing, however, was there—Hope. It was the only good the casket had held among the many evils, and it remains to this day mankind's sole comfort in misfortune.

Fiction

Step 2 Diagram the plot.

Now that you've read the myth, describe the five parts of the plot—
exposition, rising action, climax, falling action, and resolution—on a
Plot Diagram.

Directions: Complete this Plot Diagram using key events from "Pandora."

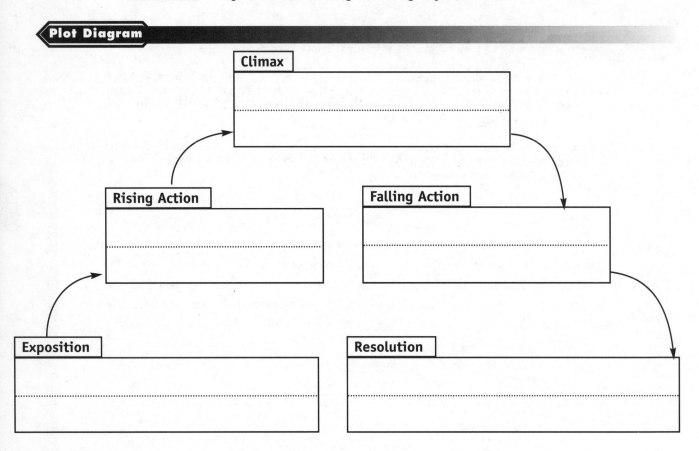

Plot Diagram

Climax

Rising Action

Falling Action

Exposition

Resolution

Step 3 Consider the climax.

The climax is the turning point in the action of a story.

Directions: Reread what you wrote on your Plot Diagram. Then, explain the
point at which the climax occurs in "Pandora."

In "Pandora," the climax occurs

....

....

....

....

Focus on  Setting

The setting affects the mood, characters, and plot of a story.

Step 1 Do a close reading.

As you read, carefully note the details of the story's setting. You usually can infer a great deal from them.

Directions: Read this paragraph. Underline any clues about time and place.

> ### from *The House of Sand and Fog* by Andre Dubus III
>
> The fat one he calls me because I am Persian and because I can bear this August sun longer than the Chinese and the Panamanians and even the little Vietnamese, Tran. He works very quickly without rest, but when Torez stops the orange highway truck in front of the crew, Tran hurries for his paper cup of water with the rest of them. This heat is no good for work. All morning we have walked this highway between Sausalito and the Golden Gate Park. We carry our small trash harpoons and we drag our burlap bags and we are dressed in vests the same color as the highway truck. Some of the Panamanians remove their shirts and leave them hanging from their back pockets like oil rags, but Torez says something to them in their mother language and he makes them wear the vests over their bare backs. We are up on a small hill. Between the trees I can see out over Sausalito to the bay where there are clouds so thick I cannot see the other side where I live with my family in Berkeley, my wife and son. But here there is no fog, only sun on your head and back, and the smell of everything under the nose: the dry grass and dirt; the cigarette smoke of the Chinese; the hot metal and exhaust of the passing automobiles. . . .

Step 2 Draw conclusions about mood and character.

The setting of a story can make you feel a certain way or give you ideas about the characters. In other words, it can affect both mood and characterization.

Directions: Read these details about the setting. Then, write your inferences about mood and character.

Inference Chart

Quotes from the Text	My Thoughts about Mood	My Thoughts about Character
I can bear this August sun longer		
All morning we have walked this highway		
But here there is no fog, only sun on your head and back		

Step 3 Make predictions.

The descriptions of the setting can help you understand the plot of a story. It will give you clues about what's to come.

Directions: Make a prediction about what you think happens next in *The House of Sand and Fog*. Then, describe how you made your prediction.

My prediction:

....

....

....

....

....

....

....

....

My reasoning:

....

....

....

....

....

....

....

....

....

....

Fiction

Focus on Characters

Some stories are more memorable for the characters than anything else. A powerful main character can drive the action and shape the themes of an entire work.

Step 1 Read for character clues.

Directions: Read this excerpt from a novel about a teenager named Sean who has been unable to voluntarily move a muscle since birth. Make notes about Sean on the sticky.

from *Stuck in Neutral* by Terry Trueman

Nobody has ever said to me, "Blink your eyes twice if you understand me," or tried to teach me Morse code so that if I could control my neck muscles I might bang out something like "Howdy, I remember everything I hear so would you mind playing a little rock and roll?" Nobody has ever held my fingers over a Ouija board or drawn letters with their fingers on my chest. Nobody's ever tried any of these Hollywood-movie techniques of making contact. They think I'm too far gone for that. But the fact is none of these things would work anyhow. They wouldn't work for me because I can't control *any* of my muscles; I've never been able to and I know that I never will. My brain just can't do it. Period. "Blink your eyes if you understand." Well, if I could, I would. I'm trying, like I've tried ten million times before, and it doesn't work; I can't control my blinks. "Bounce your head if you want some chocolate cake." I'd love some chocolate cake, but not only can I not bounce my head, I can't even chew the cake if you shove some into my mouth. I have to just let it sit there and kind of melt into chocolate mush and wait for my swallow reflex to kick in.

What I know about Sean:

....

....

....

....

....

....

....

Step 2 Make inferences.

Now, use the clues you've found to help you make inferences about the character.

Directions: Complete this inference chart about Sean.

Inference Chart

The Character's Thoughts	What I Can Conclude about Him
"Howdy, I remember everything I hear so would you mind playing a little rock and roll?"	
They think I'm too far gone for that.	
Well, if I could, I would. I'm trying, like I've tried ten million times before, and it doesn't work, I can't control my blinks.	

Step 3 Connect character to theme.

Remember that a character's thoughts and actions can often point the way to important themes in the work.

Directions: A big idea in *Stuck in Neutral* is "facing adversity." Make a connection between this idea and the character of Sean. Write your ideas on the lines.

Big idea: Facing adversity

My ideas:

Fiction

Focus on  Theme

Remember that themes are the statements about life that the author wants to convey in a story. You will find clues about themes by examining the plot and characters of a story.

Step 1 Identify the "big ideas" or central topics.

To find the central topics of a story, ask yourself, "What people, places, and things is the author talking about?"

Directions: Reread "Pandora" (which you originally read on page 135). Then write three of the myth's central topics below.

> ### "Pandora" by Edith Hamilton
>
> Another story about Pandora is that the source of all misfortune was not her wicked nature, but only her curiosity. The gods presented her with a box into which each had put something harmful, and forbade her to ever open it. Then they sent her to Epimetheus, who took her gladly although Prometheus had warned him never to accept anything from Zeus. He took her, and afterward when that dangerous thing, a woman, was his, he understood how good his brother's advice had been. For Pandora *had* to know what was in the box. One day she lifted the lid—and out flew plagues innumerable, sorrow, and mischief for mankind. In terror Pandora clapped the lid down, but too late. One good thing, however, was there—Hope. It was the only good the casket had held among the many evils, and it remains to this day mankind's sole comfort in misfortune. . . .

Central Topics

Topic #1	Topic #2	Topic #3

Step 2 Consider what the characters do and say.

Next, make a connection between the topics and the characters in the work.

Directions: Read the following quotes from "Pandora." Then explain how they relate to the big ideas in the myth.

Inference Chart

Quote	What I Think about It
Another story about Pandora is that the source of all misfortune was not her wicked nature, but only her curiosity.	
One day she lifted the lid—and out flew plagues innumerable, sorrow, and mischief for mankind.	
It was the only good the casket had held among the many evils, and it remains to this day mankind's sole comfort in misfortune.	

Step 3 Think about the point the author is making.

The theme is the point the author is making about the central topic. When trying to figure out the theme of a work you have just read, try this formula:

Central Idea + What the Author Says About the Central Topic = The Theme of the Work

Directions: Use the formula to help you find one theme in "Pandora."

....

+

....

=

....

Step 4 Pull it all together.

After you identify a theme, you need to find details in the story that support it.

Directions: Explore the theme of "hope" in the myth "Pandora." Make notes on this Topic and Theme Organizer.

Topic and Theme Organizer

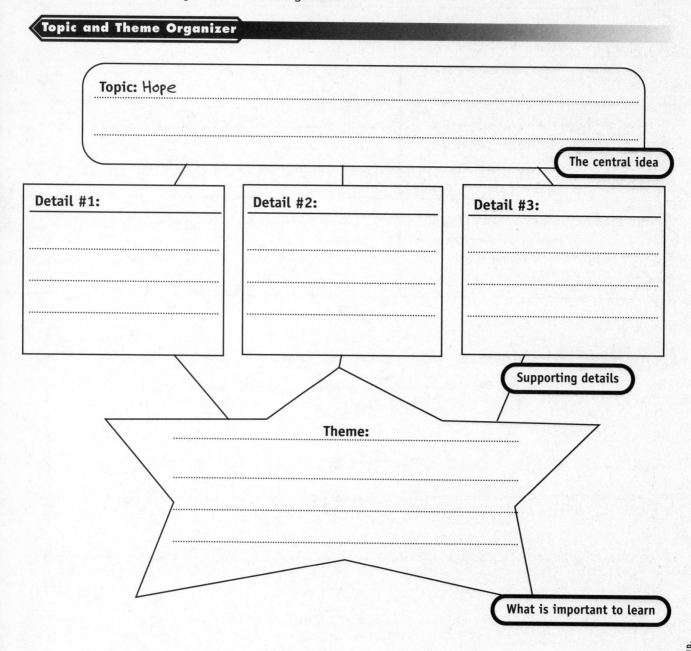

Topic: Hope

....

....

The central idea

Detail #1:

....

....

....

Detail #2:

....

....

....

Detail #3:

....

....

....

Supporting details

Theme:

....

....

....

What is important to learn

Focus on Dialogue

One of an author's main tools for telling you what a character is like is dialogue. Listen carefully to what a character is saying, and you will learn a great deal about them.

Step 1 Do a close reading.

Use the strategy of close reading to help you "hear" what the characters are saying.

__Directions:__ Carefully read this conversation between a mother and a daughter. Make notes on the stickies.

> ### from "What Means Switch" by Gish Jen
>
> . . . One day I say, "You know Ma, I have never seen a stir-fried tomato in any Chinese restaurant we have ever been in, ever."
>
> "In China," she says, real lofty, "we consider tomatoes are a delicacy."
>
> "Ma," I say. "Tomatoes are *Italian.*"
>
> "No respect for elders." She wags her finger at me, but I can tell it's just to try and shame me into believing her. "I'm tell you, tomatoes *invented* in China."
>
> "*Ma.*"
>
> "Is true. Like noodles. Invented in China."
>
> "That's not what they said in *school.*"
>
> "In *China,*" my mother counters, "we also eat tomatoes uncooked, like apple. And in summertime we slice them, and put some sugar on top."
>
> "Are you sure?"
>
> My mom says of course she's sure, and in the end I give in, even though she once told me that China was such a long time ago, a lot of things she can hardly remember.

This conversation is

between

and

They are talking

about

This is how the characters sound:

Fiction

FOR USE WITH PAGES 351–358

Step 2 Look for clues about character.

Next, make inferences about the characters based on what they said.

Directions: Write something each character says in the left column. Then, write your inferences about the character on the right.

Inference Chart

What the Says	My Inferences about the Character

What the Says	My Inferences about the Character

146

Step 3 Look for clues about mood.

Dialogue also contributes to the mood of a story.

Directions: Reread the information about dialogue and mood on page 356 of the *Reader's Handbook*. Then, describe the mood of the scene from "What Means Switch."

I think the mood is .... because ....

....

....

....

....

....

Step 4 Look for clues about plot.

Very often, dialogue can give you clues about what is going to happen next in a story.

Directions: Make a prediction of what will happen next in this story. Then explain your prediction.

My prediction: ....

....

....

I think this will happen because: ....

....

....

....

....

....

....

Focus on Comparing and Contrasting

Comparing and contrasting how two writers use the same literary element is a very common exercise.

Step 1 Read and make notes.

When comparing and contrasting two works, you need to begin by reading them both carefully with the same questions in mind. Then, choose the element you want to compare and make some notes.

Directions: Read these novel excerpts. Make notes about the two characters—Francie, in the first, and Holden, the narrator of the second.

from *A Tree Grows in Brooklyn* by Betty Smith

Francie thought that all the books in the world were in that library and she had a plan about reading all the books in the world. She was reading a book a day in alphabetical order and not skipping the dry ones. She remembered that the first author had been Abbott. She had been reading a book a day for a long time now and she was still in the B's. Already she had read about bees and buffaloes, Bermuda vacations and Byzantine architecture. For all of her enthusiasm, she had to admit that some of the B's were hard going. But Francie was a reader. She read everything she could find: trash, classics, time tables and the grocer's price list. Some of the reading had been wonderful; the Louisa Alcott books for example. She planned to read all the books over again when she had finished with the Z's.

What I can infer about Francie:

from *The Catcher in the Rye* by J. D. Salinger

Where I want to start telling is the day I left Pencey Prep. Pencey Prep is this school that's in Agerstown, Pennsylvania. You probably hear of it. You've probably seen the ads, anyway. They advertise in about a thousand magazines, always showing some hotshot guy on a horse jumping over a fence. Like as if all you ever did at Pencey was play polo all the time. I never even once saw a horse anywhere near the place. And underneath the guy on the horse's picture, it always says: "Since 1888 we have been molding boys into splendid, clear-thinking young men." Strictly for the birds. They don't do any damn more *molding* at Pencey than they do at any other school. And I didn't know anybody there that was splendid and clear-thinking at all....

What I can infer about Holden:

Step 2 Organize.

Using graphic organizers can help you sort important details in the two works.

Directions: Compare Francie and Holden on this Venn Diagram.

◁ Venn Diagram

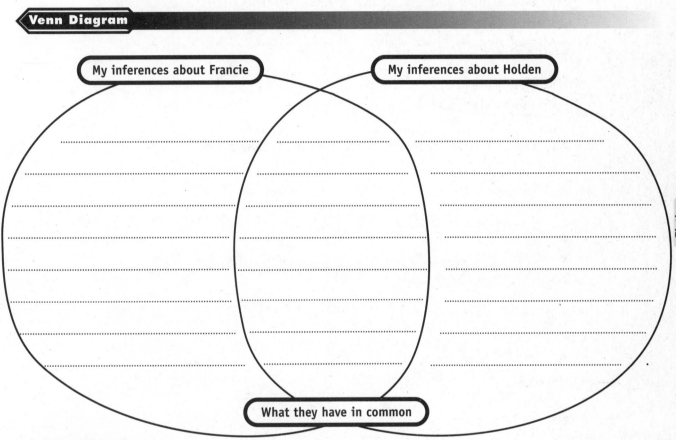

My inferences about Francie

My inferences about Holden

What they have in common

Step 3 Draw conclusions.

As a final step, draw conclusions about the similarities and differences between the two works.

Directions: Complete these two sentences.

Francie and Holden are similar in that they are both

....

....

They are different in these ways: ....

....

....

....

Fiction

Reading a Poem

Reading poetry takes time and patience but has great rewards. Good poetry readers look for meaning, listen for sounds, and try to visualize a poem's images. Use the reading process to help you get more from every poem you read.

Before Reading

Here you'll use the reading process and the strategy of close reading to help you understand and respond to a poem called "Sympathy."

 A ### Set a Purpose

Just as you do with any other type of writing, begin by setting your purpose.

• **To set your purpose, ask questions about the subject, mood, and meaning of the poem.**

Directions: Write your purpose questions for reading "Sympathy" below. Then, make a prediction about the poem.

My purpose questions:

....

....

....

....

....

My prediction:

....

....

....

Preview

Before you begin reading a poem, always spend a moment or two previewing it. This will help you get a sense of what the poem is about.

Directions: Preview "Sympathy." Then make some preview notes.

> **Preview Chart**

The title:

....

The poet's name:

....

From the background information I learned that:

....

....

The subject of the poem is:

....

....

I saw these repeated words and phrases:

....

....

Here's what I noticed about the shape and structure of the poem:

....

....

....

I noticed this about the rhyme scheme:

....

....

Poetry

Paul Laurence Dunbar (1872–1906) was the son of slaves who escaped by way of the Underground Railroad. From an early age, Paul showed talent for writing and dreamed of becoming a lawyer. Because there was no money to spare for college, however, Paul took a job as an elevator operator. When he was twenty-one years old, Paul published his first volume of poetry, which he sold to passengers who rode his elevator. Soon he had sold enough of his work that he was able to quit his job as an elevator operator and begin writing for a living. In many of his short stories and poems, Dunbar explored themes of slavery and pre-Civil War life in the South.

"Sympathy" by Paul Laurence Dunbar

I know what the caged bird feels, alas!
When the sun is bright on the upland slopes;
When the wind stirs soft through the springing grass,
And the river flows like a stream of glass;
When the first bird sings and the first bud opes,
And the faint perfume from its chalice steals— —
I know what the caged bird feels!

I know why the caged bird beats his wing
Till its blood is red on the cruel bars;
For he must fly back to his perch and cling
When he fain would be on the bough a-swing;
And a pain still throbs in the old, old scars
And they pulse again with a keener sting— —
I know why he beats his wing!

I know why the caged bird sings, ah me,
When his wing is bruised and his bosom sore— —
When he beats his bars and he would be free;
It is not a carol of joy or glee,
But a prayer that he sends from his heart's deep core,
But a plea, that upward to Heaven he flings— —
I know why the caged bird sings!

Who or what is the subject of this poem?

What is the rhyme scheme?

What is the mood?

Why do you think the poet repeats the phrase "I know why the caged bird"?

 **Plan**

After your preview, choose a strategy that can help you understand and respond to the poem.

> **• Use the strategy of close reading with poetry.**

During Reading

D **Read with a Purpose**

Plan on reading a poem several times. This way you won't have to worry about understanding everything at once.

Directions: Read "Sympathy" several times. Make notes on the organizer below.

Plan for Reading a Poem

First and Second Readings	Third and Fourth Readings	Fifth Reading
Here's what I liked about the poem:	This is what I noticed about the structure:	This is my reaction to the poem:
This is what I think the poet is saying:	This is the mood of the poem:	

Using the Strategy

Remember that close reading means reading line for line, word for word.

• Use a Double-entry Journal to keep track of your responses to words and lines in a poem.

Directions: Read the quoted lines from Dunbar's poem. Then, write what the words mean or how they make you feel.

◁ Double-entry Journal ▷

Quote	My Thoughts and Feelings
I know what the caged bird feels, alas!	
Till its blood is red on the cruel bars;	
But a plea, that upward to Heaven he flings	

Understanding How Poems Are Organized

Good poets know that the organization or structure of a poem can contribute to its meaning. For example, a poet will use rhyme to create a certain effect or repetition to draw attention to a certain idea.

Directions: Go back and reread Dunbar's poem. Think about how it sounds and looks. Make notes on the stickies that are provided.

E Connect

Making a personal connection to a poem will help you understand it. This in turn will enhance your enjoyment of the work.

• Connect to a poem by recording your thoughts and feelings about both the sound and meaning of the work.

Directions: Reflect on Dunbar's poem. Then complete the following sentences.

Connection Comments

When I read the poem, I felt:

_____

_____

I felt this because:

_____

_____

How the speaker of the poem feels about slavery:

I know this because:

_____

_____

Poetry

After Reading

When you finish reading, take a moment or two to think about what you did and did not understand about a poem.

F Pause and Reflect

Never leave a poem until you're sure you understand what all of it means.

- **After you finish a poem, ask yourself, "Have I answered my purpose questions?"**

Directions: Circle one of the answers below. Then explain your answer.

I feel I have / have not met my reading purpose. Here's why:

_____

_____

G Reread

Once you understand a poem, you can relax and enjoy it. "Listen" to the rhythm of the verse. Think about the message the poet has for you.

- **A powerful rereading strategy to use with poetry is paraphrasing.**

Directions: Reread Dunbar's poem one last time. Then, make notes in the Paraphrase Chart below.

Paraphrase Chart

Lines from the Poem	My Paraphrase
When the first bird sings and the first bud opes	
I know why the caged bird beats his wing/ Till its blood is red on the cruel bars	
It is not a carol of joy or glee,/ But a prayer that he sends from his heart's deep core	

 Remember

When you finish reading, do a little writing. It will help you better remember what you've read.

• **Writing can help you remember a poem's subject and meaning.**

Directions: Write a letter in which you describe "Sympathy" and what it meant to you.

Letter

NAME ....

Focus on  Language

*In most cases when reading a poem, it's the language—
the individual words and phrases—that captures your
attention first.*

Step 1 Read for key words.

On your first or second reading of a poem, watch for key words, especially
words that describe an action, create a mood, or name a person, place,
or thing.

Directions: Read "The Tyger." Underline words that grab your attention.
Then, make notes on the stickies.

> ### "The Tyger" by William Blake
>
> Tyger! Tyger! burning bright!
> In the forests of the night,
> What immortal hand or eye
> Could frame thy fearful symmetry?
>
> In what distant deeps or skies
> Burnt the fire of thine eyes?
> On what wings dare he aspire?
> What the hand dare seize the fire?
>
> And what shoulder, and what art,
> Could twist the sinews of thy heart?
> And when thy heart began to beat,
> What dread hand and what dread feet?
>
> What the hammer? what the chain?
> In what furnace was thy brain?
> What the anvil? what dread grasp
> Dare its deadly terrors clasp?
>
> When the stars threw down their spears,
> And watered heaven with their tears,
> Did He smile His work to see?
> Did He who made the Lamb, make thee?

> What is the subject
> of the poem?

Poetry

"The Tyger" by William Blake

Tyger! Tyger! burning bright,
In the forests of the night,
What immortal hand or eye
Dare frame thy fearful symmetry?

How does the poet feel about the subject?

Step 2 Think about word connotations.

Connotation is the feeling conveyed by a word. The connotation of the words in a poem can also point toward its meaning.

Directions: Read the words in the left-hand column. Write their connotations on the right.

Word Connotations

Words from the Poem	Feelings They Convey
burning, immortal, fearful, seize, dread, anvil, deadly	

Step 3 Look for figurative language, imagery, and repetition.

Figurative language, imagery, and repetition give depth and meaning to a poem.

Directions: Look at the examples of imagery in "The Tyger" in the chart on the next page. Write down in the chart what you think the phrases mean and what sense or senses you use to experience the words. Then, make notes about repetition in the poem.

Imagery Chart

Imagery from the Poem	What I Think It Means	The Sense or Senses I Use
In the forests of the night		
What the hand dare seize the fire?		

These words are repeated in "The Tyger":

The repetition tells me that

Step 4 Consider the tone and mood.

As a final step, think about the tone and mood of the poem.

<u>**Directions:**</u> Record your thoughts about tone and mood in a journal entry.

Journal

Poetry

Focus on Meaning

As you've seen, close reading is the best way to read and understand a poem. Follow these steps to get at the exact meaning.

Step 1 Examine the poem's language.

First, read the poem the whole way through without stopping. Then examine individual words.

Directions: Read this excerpt from a poem. Circle words that seem interesting or important. Then, make notes on the sticky.

from " 'For oh,' say the children, 'we are weary' " by Elizabeth Barrett Browning

"For oh," say the children, "we are weary
And we cannot run or leap;
If we cared for any meadows, it were merely
To drop down in them and sleep.
Our knees tremble sorely in the stooping,
We fall upon our faces, trying to go;
And underneath our heavy eyelids drooping
The reddest flower would look as pale as snow.
For, all day, we drag our burden tiring
Through the coal-dark, underground;
Or, all day, we drive the wheels of iron
In the factories, round and round. . . ."

What would you say is the connotation of the words weary, stooping, drooping, and coal-dark?
....
....

What is the effect of these words?
....
....
....

Step 2 Think about the poet's style.

Style is how the author uses language. Some of the many stylistic elements are figurative language, imagery, rhythm, and word choice.

Directions: Think about the style of Browning's poem. Then, complete this Double-entry Journal.

Double-entry Journal

Browning's Words	My Thoughts
pale as snow	
coal-dark underground	
heavy eyelids drooping	

Step 3 Reflect on the poet's attitude.

This formula can help you find the message of a poem:

topic of the poem   +   what the poet is saying about the topic   =   the poet's message

Directions: Use the formula to find Browning's message in "'For oh,' say the children, 'We are weary.'"

Poetry

Subject of the poem	+	What Browning says	=	The poet's message
	+		**=**	

Step 4 Listen to your own feelings.

Ask yourself, "How does the poem make me feel?"

Directions: Write your feelings about Browning's poem.

The poem makes me feel .... because ....

....

....

....

....

....

....

....

Focus on Sound and Structure

Sound and structure are yet more elements of a poem for you to understand. To focus on sound and structure, examine how the poem looks, and listen to how it sounds.

Step 1 Do a careful reading.

First, read the poem the whole way through without stopping. Then make some notes about how it looks and sounds.

Directions: Read this poem by Thomas Hardy. Make notes on the stickies.

"Throwing a Tree" by Thomas Hardy

The two executioners stalk along over the knolls,
Bearing two axes with heavy heads shining and wide,
And a long limp two-handled saw toothed for cutting great boles,
And so they approach the prod tree that bears the death-mark on its side.

Jackets doffed they swing axes and chop away just above the ground,
And the chips fly about and lie white on the moss and fallen leaves;
Till a broad deep gash in the bark is hewn all the way round,
And one of them tries to hook upward a rope, which at last he achieves.

The saw then begins, till the top of the tall giant shivers:
The shivers are seen to grow greater each cut than before:
They edge out the saw, tug the rope; but the tree only quivers,
And kneeling and sawing again, they step back to try pulling once more.

Then, lastly, the living mast sways, further sways: with a shout
Job and Ike rush aside. Reached the end of its long staying powers
The tree crashes downward: it shakes all its neighbours throughout,
And two hundred years' steady growth has been ended in less than two hours.

How many stanzas does the poem have?

How many lines are there per stanza?

What do you notice about the rhyme?

What do you notice about the final line of each stanza?

Which repeated words grabbed your attention?

Poetry

Step 2 Examine the organization.

The organization of a poem can offer clues about its meaning.

Directions: Reread "Throwing a Tree,"and then summarize each stanza of Hardy's poem. Write your notes on this chart.

Stanza-by-Stanza Summary

Stanza	My Summary
1	
2	
3	
4	

Step 3 Listen for repeated sounds.

Next, listen to the "music" of the poem. What do the words sound like? What do they remind you of? What effect do they create?

Directions: Look for examples of repetition, alliteration, and assonance in "Throwing a Tree." If you need help with these terms, see pages 418–419 in the *Reader's Handbook.*

Poetic Sounds Chart

Repeated words:

Stanza	Alliteration (repeated consonant sounds)	Assonance (repeated vowel sounds)
1		
2		
3		
4		

Step 4 Explore the rhyme and rhythm.

Poets use rhyme and rhythm for many reasons, including:

• to establish a mood

• to bring emphasis to an idea

• to keep the reader interested and enhance his or her enjoyment

Directions: Answer the following questions about the rhyme and rhythm in "Throwing a Tree."

Rhyme and Rhythm Questions

1. What is the rhyme scheme in Hardy's poem?

....

2. Does it change from stanza to stanza?

....

....

3. What is the meter of the poem?

....

....

4. At what point does the meter change? What is the effect of this change?

....

....

Step 5 Put it all together.

As a final step, use your notes about sound and structure to help you make inferences about the meaning of the poem.

Directions: Use this Double-entry Journal to organize your thoughts about the meaning of Hardy's poem.

Double-entry Journal

What I Know about the Sound and Structure	My Thoughts and Ideas

Poetry

Reading a Play

A play is different from a story in that the action in a play is told entirely through the dialogue and stage directions. Your job as a reader is to listen carefully to what each character says and visualize what the characters are doing and describing.

Before Reading

Use the reading process and the strategy of summarizing to get more from every play you read. Practice here with an excerpt from *Oedipus the King* by Sophocles.

 A **Set a Purpose**

Your purpose will be the same no matter what play you are reading.

• **To set your purpose, ask questions about the setting, characters, conflict, and theme of the play.**

Directions: Write your purpose for reading *Oedipus the King* below. Then write what you already know about this play.

Purpose Questions: ....

....

....

....

....

....

What I know about the play: ....

....

....

....

B Preview

Be sure to preview a play before you begin reading. Look for both setting and character clues. Try to get a sense of what the play is about.

Directions: Preview the title page for *Oedipus the King*. Make notes on the stickies.

from *Oedipus the King* by Sophocles

ARGUMENT

To Laius, King of Thebes, an oracle foretold that the child born to him by his queen Jocasta would slay his father and wed his mother. So when in time a son was born the infant's feet were tied together and he was left to die on Mount Cithaeron. But a shepherd found the babe and saved him, and delivered him to another shepherd who took him to his master, the King of Corinth. Polybus being childless adopted the boy, who grew up believing that he was indeed the king's son. Afterwards doubting his parentage he inquired of the Delphic god and heard himself the weird oracle foretold before to Laius. So Oedipus fled from what he deemed his father's house and in his flight he encountered and unwillingly slew his father Laius. Arriving at Thebes he answered the riddle of the Sphinx and the grateful Thebans made their deliverer king. So he reigned in the room of Laius and married Jocasta, the widowed queen. Children were born to them and Thebes prospered under his rule, but again a grievous plague fell upon the city. Again the oracle was consulted and it bade them purge themselves of blood-guiltiness. Oedipus denounces the crime of which he is unaware, and undertakes to track out the criminal. Step by step it is brought home to him that he is the man. The closing scene reveals Jocasta slain by her own hand and Oedipus blinded by his own act and praying for death or exile.

DRAMATIS PERSONAE
Oedipus.
The Priest of Zeus.
Creon.
Chorus of Theban Elders.
Teiresias.
Jocasta.
Messenger.
Herd of Laius.
Second Messenger.

SETTING
Time: 430 B.C.
Place: Thebes

This is what I learned from the "Argument":
....
....
....
....
....
....
....

The setting is
....

There are
....

characters.

Drama

from *Oedipus the King* by Sophocles

SCENE 2: *Thebes. Before the palace of Oedipus.*
[Enter TEIRESIAS, led by a boy.]

OEDIPUS. Teiresias, seer who understands all of heaven and earth, although thou
blinded eyes see nothing. A plague infects our city; and we turn to thee, O seer, as
our only hope. The messengers have no doubt told thee—how we have but one
choice, and that is to find Laius's murderers and deal with them. Then and only
then will we find relief from our suffering. Therefore, tell us all, and keep nothing
from us, so that you may save thyself, thy country, and thy king, and all that is
touched by this deadly disease. We put our hopes on you, Teiresias. This is man's
highest end, to others' service all his powers to lend.

TEIRESIAS. Alas, alas, what misery it is to be wise, when wisdom can do no good!
But how horrible this old story is, and how long I have forgotten it. I should not
have come.

OEDIPUS. But why? What ails thee? Why this melancholy mood?

TEIRESIAS. Let me go home—prevent me not.

OEDIPUS. For shame! No true-born Theban patriot would refuse to answer!

TEIRESIAS. I see danger in thy words, O king, and I shall not add to it.

OEDIPUS. Oh speak, and withhold nothing, I beg you; if you can answer, then you

Stop and Organize

What is Oedipus saying here? Make notes on the Character Map on page 170.

TEIRESIAS. But you are blind! No! I shall not reveal my secrets, and nor will I
reveal yours!

OEDIPUS. What then? You know and yet will not speak? Is it possible that you
would betray us and the city in such a way?

TEIRESIAS. I will not cause you further grief, and I will not grieve myself. Why do
you ask me such questions when you have no desire to learn?

OEDIPUS. Monster! Your silence would anger a rock. Will nothing loosen your
tongue? Can nothing move you, or shake loose the truth from your lips?

TEIRESIAS. You blame my mood, and see not yourself. Know yourself, Oedipus. You
denounce me, but you know nothing of yourself.

OEDIPUS. You expect me to control my rage after you have disgraced your city?
How do you dare?

TEIRESIAS. But it does not matter if I speak. The future will come—it has already

from *Oedipus the King* by Sophocles

been set and cannot be changed.

OEDIPUS. Since come it must, your duty is to tell me.

Stop and Organize
How does Teiresias feel about Oedipus? Make notes on the Character Map on page 170.

OEDIPUS. Yes, I am enraged, and I will not be careful with my words—I will speak my whole mind and tell you what I think. I think this horrible crime was *your* doing. You did everything except commit the murder itself, and you would have done *that* had you not been blind! It is you who has done this bloody deed!

TEIRESIAS. Is that the truth? Then I ask you to listen to your own proclamation. From this day forward, deny yourself the right to speak to me or anyone. For it is you, Oedipus. You are the polluter of this land.

OEDIPUS. Vile slanderer! How dare you blame me? Do you think that you can tell these lies and then go free?

TEIRESIAS. Yea, I am free. I remain strong, with truth as my protector.

OEDIPUS. But who told you this? It came from no prophecy—I know that to be true.

TEIRESIAS. It is *you* who taught me. You forced me to say this, against my will.

OEDIPUS. Then say your speech again. I want no doubt in my mind.

TEIRESIAS. Are you trying to provoke me to more anger? Is that your aim?

OEDIPUS. No. I only half caught your meaning. I want to hear it all again so that I am sure.

TEIRESIAS. I say *you* are the murderer of Laius. You are the murderer that you have been searching for!

OEDIPUS. But again! You have said this again, and in repeating it have made yet a larger mistake.

TEIRESIAS. Shall I tell you more? You are angry enough to hear.

OEDIPUS. Say what you will. It will all be a waste of breath.

TEIRESIAS. I say you live in shame with your nearest kin. Without knowing it, you commit the ugliest of sins.

OEDIPUS. Do you think I will allow you to speak like this forever?

TEIRESIAS. If the truth is to prevail, then I shall be permitted to speak.

OEDIPUS. Other men speak the truth. But you—you are a fool. You are blind, you

Stop and Organize
How does Oedipus act in this scene? Make notes on the Character Map on page 170.

Drama

> **from *Oedipus the King* by Sophocles**

TEIRESIAS. You're a fool to insult me for telling the truth. One day you will know that
I've told no lies.

OEDIPUS. You are a man of the endless night, Teiresias. And so you cannot hurt me,
just as you cannot hurt any man who sees the light.

TEIRESIAS. True, it is not I that will cause your downfall. I leave that to the god Apollo.

OEDIPUS. Was this a trick from Creon—or was it your own?

TEIRESIAS. No, not Creon, and not my own. You destroy your own self, Oedipus.

C Plan

After your preview, make a plan. Choose a strategy that can help you
understand the characters, actions, and themes of the play.

- **Use the strategy of summarizing to help you keep track of important
elements in a play.**

During Reading

D Read with a Purpose

There are several different tools that you can use with the strategy of
summarizing. One that works particularly well is a Character Map.

Directions: Do a careful reading of the argument and scene 2 from *Oedipus
the King*. Make notes about Oedipus on the Character Map.

> **Character Map**

What the character says and does	What others think about the character

Oedipus

How the character acts and feels	How I feel about the character

Using the Strategy

Use a Magnet Summary to explore the big ideas you find in a play. These big ideas may point the way to important themes.

Directions: An important idea in Oedipus is "blindness." Skim the excerpt to see how many mentions of being blind or blindness you find. Then, complete this Magnet Summary.

◄ **Magnet Summary**

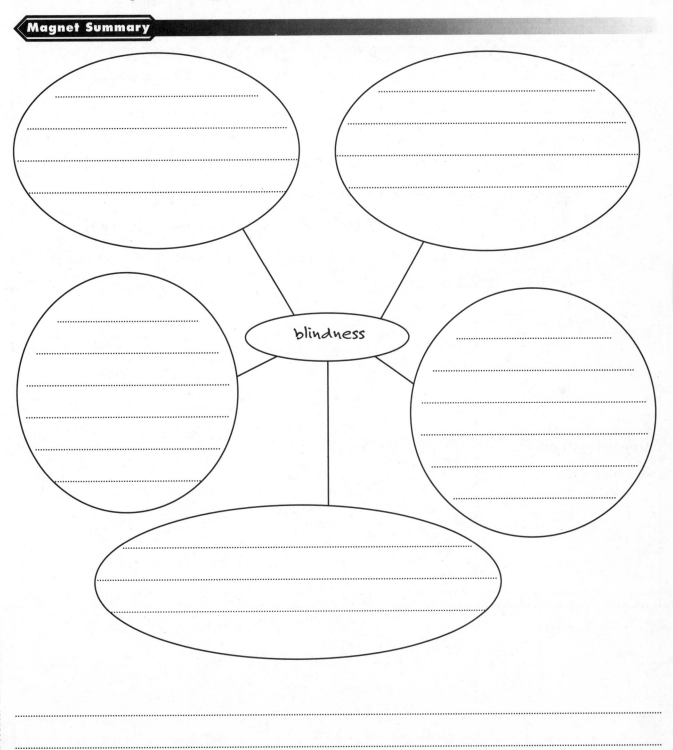

blindness

Drama

Understanding How Plays Are Organized

Plays are divided into acts and scenes. Each act or scene moves the characters closer to the climax of the plot.

• **Make a scene-by-scene summary to keep track of what happens in a play. Reread what you've written if you find yourself lost.**

Directions: Read the summary for Scene 1 of *Oedipus the King*. Then write a summary for Scene 2.

Scene-by-Scene Summary

Part of Play	Setting	Key Events
Scene 1	outside the palace at Thebes	The citizens of Thebes beg Oedipus to rid the city of the plague. Oedipus explains that he sent his brother-in-law, Creon, to the oracle at Delphi to get help. Creon returns and tells Oedipus that the only way to stop the plague is for Oedipus to find and banish the murderer of King Laius.
Scene 2		

Connect

Making a personal connection to a play can help you think more critically about what you've read.

• **Connect to a play by recording your thoughts and feelings about the characters and action.**

Directions: Reread this short speech from *Oedipus the King*. Then write your reaction.

> OEDIPUS. Yes, I am enraged, and I will not be careful with my words—I will speak my whole mind and tell you what I think. I think this horrible crime was *your* doing. You did everything except commit the murder itself, and you would have done *that* had you not been blind! It is you who has done this bloody deed!

I think Oedipus is ....

because ....

....

....

....

After Reading

When you finish a play, think about what you've learned.

 Pause and Reflect

Ask yourself about the characters, setting, conflict, and theme.

• **Always check to see if you've met your original reading purpose.**

Directions: How well did you meet your reading purpose? What would you like to find out more about? Explain here.

....
....
....
....
....
....

Drama

Reread

An important part of reading a play is visualizing the action. This can be very helpful if you are having a hard time understanding what happens in a particular scene.

- **A powerful rereading strategy to use is visualizing and thinking aloud. It can help you "see" important ideas in the play.**

Directions: Draw a picture of Oedipus and Teiresias in front of the palace of Thebes. Then, write a caption that summarizes what is happening.

Sketch

| |
| |
| |
| |
| |

H **Remember**

It is important to find a way to remember what you've read.

- **Performing an oral reading of a key scene can help you recall important elements of the play.**

Directions: Choose a short passage from *Oedipus the King*. Write the passage here. Then, get together with a partner and discuss why you chose this particular passage.

Passage from Oedipus the King:

....

....

....

....

....

Why I chose this passage:

....

Focus on Language

Focusing on dramatic language means analyzing the key lines and speeches, stage directions, and the dialogue between characters in a play. Follow these steps.

Step 1 Examine key lines and speeches.

When you read a play, always keep an eye out for the key lines and speeches. They will give you important clues about a character's personality.

Directions: Read this speech from *Oedipus the King*. Then, write adjectives that describe Teiresias on the sticky.

---

from *Oedipus the King* by Sophocles

TEIRESIAS. I will go when I've said all that I came to say. I am not afraid of you. You cannot hurt me. And I tell you this: The man you seek—the man whose death or banishment you ordered, the man who murdered Laius—that man is here, living in our midst. Soon it will be known to all of you—he is a native Thebian. And he will find no joy in that discovery. His eyes now see, but soon they will be blind; rich now, but soon a beggar. . . .

Adjectives that describe

Teiresias:

_____

_____

_____

_____

_____

Step 2 Read the stage directions.

Reading the stage directions makes it easier for you to visualize the action of a play. They can give you clues about setting and action.

Drama

Directions: Read these stage directions from Scene 1 of *Oedipus the King*. Make notes on the stickies.

Scene: *In front of the doors at the palace of Oedipus at Thebes. A crowd of citizens sits at an altar in supplication. Among them is an old man, the priest of Zeus.*

Where does the opening scene take place?

Who is there?

Step 3 Analyze the dialogue.

Dialogue can point the way to a play's theme.

Directions: Read this conversation between Oedipus and a shepherd who knows the truth about the king. Look for a line that supports Sophocles' theme of blindness. Write the line in the organizer and then explain what it means.

from *Oedipus the King* by Sophocles

OEDIPUS. But this prophecy! What was it, good Shephard?

SHEPHERD. The prophecy said that the child would kill his father.

OEDIPUS. Then why did you give the baby away? Why did you not kill it?

SHEPHERD. I felt sorry for him, master. And I thought that he would take the babe to his own home. But he saved the babe from his suffering—for worse suffering yet. My Lord, if you are the man he says you are—O god—you were born for suffering!

OEDIPUS. O God! O no! I see it now! All clear! O Light! I will never look on you again! Sin! Sin in my birth! Sin in my marriage! Sin in blood!

Double-entry Journal

Quote	My Thoughts

NAME ....

Focus on (Theme)

The theme of a play is the writer's message. Use this three-step plan to find and evaluate a playwright's theme.

Step 1 Look for repeated words and symbols.

First, look for repeated words and symbols in a play. Some of these will point to the general topics the playwright is exploring.

Directions: Think about the key words and symbols in *Oedipus the King*. Write them on the Web below.

◀ **Web**

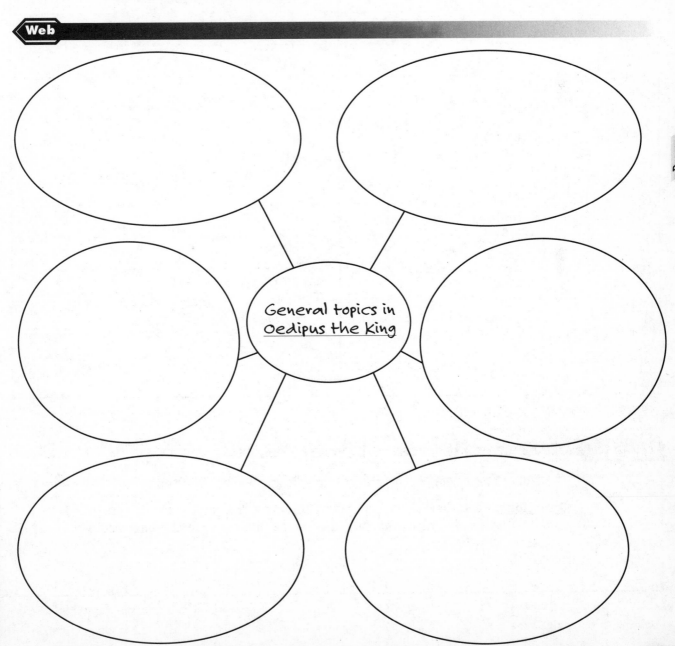

General topics in
<u>Oedipus the King</u>

Drama

Step 2 Note what the characters say and do.

Next, think about what the characters say and do that relate to these general topics.

Directions: Choose one general topic from your Web to explore. Write what Oedipus and Teiresias say about the topic.

General Topic:	
What Oedipus Says	**What Teiresias Says**
calls	
says	calls

Step 3 Write a theme statement.

Remember that theme is the playwright's message about the topic.

Directions: Read the information about finding a theme on page 483 in the *Reader's Handbook*. Then, complete the Theme Organizer on the next page.

NAME

Theme Organizer

Topic:

Detail #1:

Detail #2:

Detail #3:

Theme:

Drama

Focus on Shakespeare

The reading process and the strategy of using graphic organizers can help you read, understand, and respond to the plays by William Shakespeare.

Step 1 Read for sense.

First, read a passage once or twice. Use context clues and the footnotes to help you with difficult words.

Directions: Read this passage from *A Midsummer Night's Dream*. In this scene, a young man named Lysander speaks to Hermia, the woman he loves.

from *A Midsummer Night's Dream* by William Shakespeare

LYSANDER: . . . hear me, Hermia.
I have a widow aunt, a dowager
Of great revenue, and she hath no child.
From Athens is her house remote seven leagues;
And she respects me as her only son.   5
There, gentle Hermia, may I marry thee,
And to that place the sharp Athenian law
Cannot pursue us. If thou lovest me, then,
Steal forth thy father's house tomorrow night;
And in the wood, a league without the town,   10
Where I did meet thee once with Helena
To do observance to a morn of May,
There will I stay for thee.

---

5 **respects** regards

11 **without** outside

> This is what Lysander is saying to Hermia:
> ....
> ....
> ....
> ....

Step 2 Read for specifics.

When you read for specifics, you read to understand the important literary elements of the work. Using graphic organizers can help.

Directions: Read the text in the left-hand column. Write what it tells you about Lysander on the right.

◄ **Inference Chart**

Text	What It Tells Me About the Character
There, gentle Hermia, may I marry thee,	
Steal forth thy father's house tomorrow night;	

Step 3 Reflect.

Reacting or making personal connections to a Shakespearean play can heighten your enjoyment of the work. It can also help you think critically about the action, characters, or scene.

Directions: Reflect on the experiences you have had reading Shakespeare. Then, explain what you enjoy about his work and what makes it challenging for you.

When I read Shakespeare, I enjoy

This is what I find challenging

Drama

Reading a Website

Always read a website with a critical eye. Zero in on the information you need, and then double-check to see if it's reliable.

Before Reading

Practice using the reading process and the strategy of reading critically with a website designed for sports fans.

 A   Set a Purpose

It's easy to lose your way on the Internet. One false click, and you're lost in a jungle of unfamiliar websites. To prevent this from happening, set your purpose *before* accessing a website.

• **To set your purpose, make a list of questions about the subject.**

<u>Directions:</u> Use this K-W-L Chart to record your areas of expertise when it comes to sports. Then, write what you want to find out.

K-W-L Chart

What I Know	What I Want to Know	What I Learned

Preview

It's vitally important that you preview a website before you begin clicking. This will give you a sense of what's offered and whether or not the site can help you meet your purpose.

Directions: Preview the sports fan website that follows. Check each item on this checklist. Make notes about what you find.

Preview Checklist

Preview Checklist	My Notes
❏ The name and overall look of the site	
❏ The main menu or table of contents	
❏ The source or sponsor	
❏ Any descriptions of the site	
❏ Any images or graphics that create a feeling	
❏ The purpose of the site	

Internet

http://www.sportsfans.com/home.asp*

The National Sports Association presents

SportsFans.com

Subscribers log in here

Click here for

MLB

NFL

NHL

NBA

NCAA Football

NCAA Basketball

PGA/WPGA

NASCAR

World Cup Tennis

Wrestling

Additional sports

SportsFans.com has been entertaining sports fans since 1993. This is your site for what's new, what's hot, and what's coming up in the world of sports. Here you can read about your favorite teams, your favorite leagues, and your favorite players. Our mission is to present equal and fair coverage of every team playing today in the professional and semi-professional leagues.

Fans are talking about . . .

The Final Four

Baseball's Season Openers

Looking Ahead to the Indy 500

<u>click here</u> for more on these subjects

SportsFans.com is a project of the National Sports Clearinghouse, an affiliate of Bear Creek University in Bear Creek, New York. Coach Jamelle Walber is director of this site. Direct your comments to Coach Walber at www.jwalber@sfs.com/.

This site is updated daily.
Last updated: August 23, 2003

*URL is not real.

C Plan

Next, make a reading plan. Choose a strategy that can help you read and evaluate the information offered on the site. The strategy of reading critically may be your best choice.

- **Reading critically means asking yourself, "How much can I trust this website?"**

During Reading

D Read with a Purpose

Keep in mind your purpose questions as you examine the site. Remember that you want to find reliable information about the given topic. Use a Website Profiler to organize your notes.

Directions: Read the sportsfans.com website carefully. Make notes on the following Website Profiler.

Website Profiler

URL	
Sponsor	Date
Point of View	Expertise
Reaction/Evaluation	

Internet

Using the Strategy

Before you can evaluate the information on a website, you also need to note the links it has to offer and if they are up-to-date. Use Study Cards to keep track of worthwhile links.

- **When you read critically, you keep track of which links can help you meet your purpose.**

Directions: Make notes about the sportsfans.com website on these Study Cards. Tell which links you should follow and explain why.

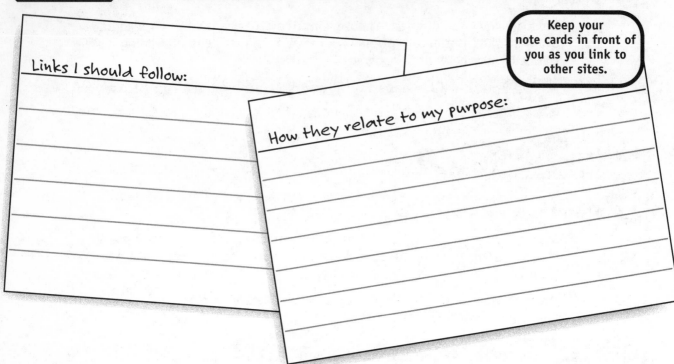

Links I should follow:

How they relate to my purpose:

Keep your note cards in front of you as you link to other sites.

Understanding How Websites Are Organized

A website looks like what it is called: a Web.

- **Map a website by creating a Web showing the links from the home page.**

Directions: Complete this Web. List three important links on the website. Predict what you think you'll find there.

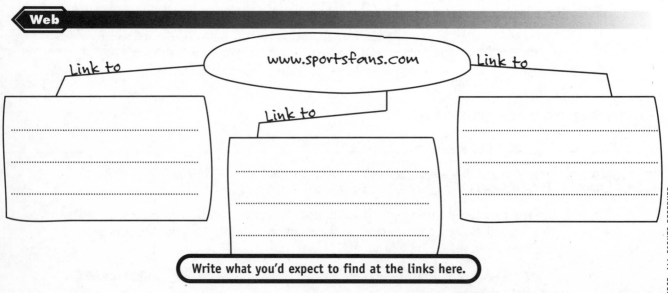

Link to

www.sportsfans.com

Link to

Link to

Write what you'd expect to find at the links here.

E **Connect**

To get everything you can out of a website, think about how its ideas and content apply to you. An important part of this is deciding whether or not you want to return to the site again in the future.

> • **Be sure to consider whether the website was of use to you personally.**

Directions: Think of two websites you've visited recently. Explain your opinion of each site and why you will or will not return.

◄ **Connecting to a Website**

> Website #1
> ....
> My opinion of it:
> ....
> ....
> ....
> Why I will or will not return:
> ....
> ....

> Website #2
> ....
> My opinion of it:
> ....
> ....
> Why I will or will not return:
> ....
> ....

Internet

After Reading

When you finish reading, take a moment or two to think about what you did and did not understand about the website. If the site has been helpful, make sure your notes are in good order before moving the mouse.

 F **Pause and Reflect**

First, recall your original purpose for visiting the site.

> • **As you finish using a website, ask yourself, "How well did I meet my purpose? Is there anything else I need to learn?"**

Directions: Return to the K-W-L Chart on page 182 and complete the "L" column. Then, make some additional notes about the sportsfans.com site here.

I need to find out more about:
....
....

Reread

There will be times that you'll want to return to a website to check a fact
or search for additional information. Other times, you may want to evaluate
the site as a whole. In both cases, the strategy of skimming can help.

• **Use the rereading strategy of skimming when checking the reliability
of the information posted on a website.**

Directions: Read these questions. Skim the sportsfans.com website
for answers.

Evaluating Internet Sources

1. Was the site updated recently? How often is it updated?	2. What is the source of the site?	3. What credentials does the site offer?	4. Are there any obvious errors on the site?

These are the questions you should ask yourself when evaluating a website.

 Remember

Recording information on a graphic organizer can help you remember
information from a website.

• **Use a graphic organizer to help you remember key elements of a website.**

Directions: Complete this graphic organizer about the sportsfans.com
website.

Source Evaluator

Research Purpose	
Title or Location	
Date	
Expertise	
Bias, if any	
Reactions	

Reading a

Graphics are visual representations of information. Your job when reading a graphic is to understand the information presented and then figure out why it is important. The reading process can help.

Before Reading

Use the reading process and the strategy of summarizing to help you read and respond to a graphic about electricity usage.

 A Set a Purpose

Most graphics contain words as well as visuals. Set a purpose that can help explore all of the elements of the graphic.

• **To set your purpose, ask two or more questions about the graphic.**

Directions: Write your purpose for reading a line graph that shows the number of kilowatt hours used each year from 1989 to 2001. Then make a prediction.

Purpose question #1: ....

....

....

Purpose question #2: ....

....

....

My prediction: ....

....

....

Internet

B Preview

When you preview, ask yourself, "What is the big picture shown in this graphic?" Try to get a sense of what information is being offered, how it is organized, and why it might be important.

Directions: Preview the line graph shown below. Then, make some preview notes.

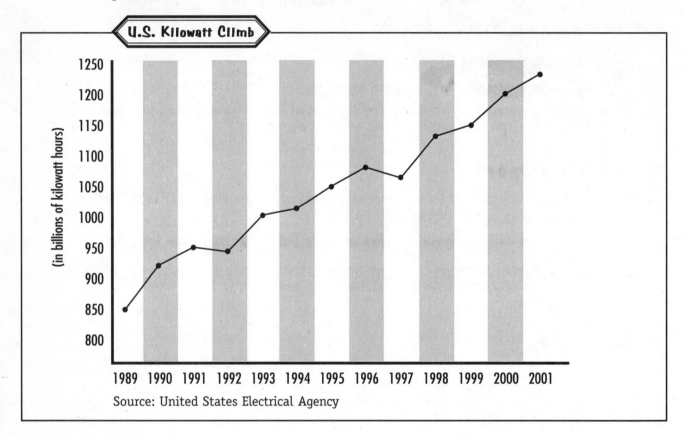

U.S. Kilowatt Climb

Source: United States Electrical Agency

Title of the graphic: ....

Type of graphic: ....

Dates represented: ....

Labels, column and row headings: ....

....

....

What is the big picture? ....

....

....

 **Plan**

Your next step is to make a plan. Choose a strategy that will help you read, interpret, and respond to the graphic.

• **The strategy of paraphrasing works well with most graphics because it can help you process the key facts and details.**

During Reading

Remember that in a graphic, the visual element and the text are equally important.

D **Read with a Purpose**

Reread the plan for reading a graphic on page 544 of the *Reader's Handbook*. Use this plan to interpret the kilowatt-hour line graph.

Directions: Read the kilowatt-hour line graph. Then paraphrase, or tell in your own words, what the graphic shows. Write your paraphrase on the lines below.

What the graphic shows:

....

....

....

....

....

....

....

Graphics

Using the Strategy

When you paraphrase, you take key details from a text and put them in your own words. Using your own words can help you process and remember what you've read. A Paraphrase Chart can help.

Directions: Complete this Paraphrase Chart using information from the kilowatt graphic. See page 545 of the *Reader's Handbook* if you're not sure how to use this tool.

Paraphrase Chart

Title	"Kilowatt Climb"
My Paraphrase	
My Thoughts	

NAME ....

Understanding How Graphics Are Organized

Familiarize yourself with the key elements used in graphics. This will make it easier for you to read all the different types of graphics.

Directions: Label the following elements on the graphic below: *title, source, horizontal (x) axis,* and *vertical (y) axis.*

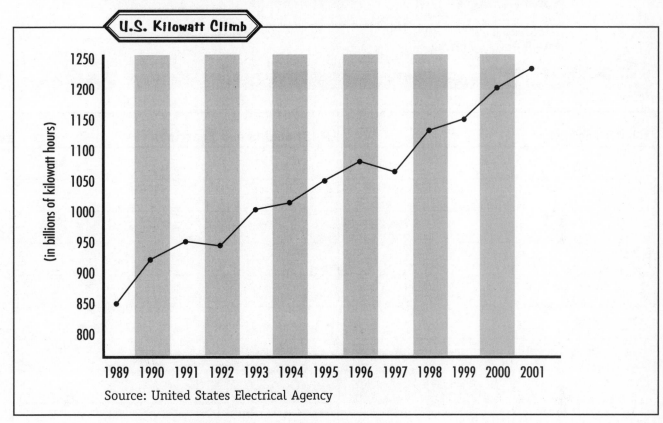

U.S. Kilowatt Climb

(in billions of kilowatt hours)

Source: United States Electrical Agency

Graphics

1. How many kilowatt hours were used by Americans in 1989?
....

2. How many additional kilowatt hours were used in 1990?
....

3. What do you notice about the years 1992 and 1997?
....

....

....

4. What would you predict would be the total kilowatt usage in 2002 using this graphic as evidence?
....

....

....

....

....

....

Connect

Understanding why the information in a graphic is important—and what it means to you personally—is an important part of reading critically.

- **To connect to a graphic, ask yourself, "What does the information mean to me?"**

Directions: Record your thoughts about the electricity graphic on this Double-entry Journal.

Double-Entry Journal

What I Learned	My Thoughts and Reactions

 **After Reading**

Make it a habit to return to a graphic to be sure you haven't missed anything.

 Pause and Reflect

First, go back to your reading purpose.

> • **After you read a graphic, ask yourself, "How well did I meet my purpose? Is there anything else I need to learn?"**

Directions: Answer your reading purpose questions.

What is the graphic about?
....

What does it show me?
....

....

....

What conclusions can I draw from the graphic?
....

....

....

 Reread

Good readers are skeptical about the information presented. They don't automatically trust that everything they read is true.

> • **Use the rereading strategy of reading critically to help you decide whether the information in a graphic is valid.**

Directions: Take another look at the electricity graphic. Then, complete the Critical Reading Chart on the next page.

Graphics

Critical Reading Chart

"Kilowatt Climb"	
1. What is being compared?	
2. What similarities and differences do I see?	
3. Is there anything unusual about the way the information is presented?	
4. What trends or other relationships do I see?	

H Remember

Putting into words the main idea of a graphic can help you remember what you've seen and learned.

• **Summary Notes are a way of helping you bring together the most important parts of a text.**

<u>**Directions:**</u> Write Summary Notes about the electricity graphic.

Summary Notes

Title or topic:

Main point:

Smaller, related points:

1.

2.

3.

Reading a Driver's Handbook

It is very important that you read your driver's handbook slowly and carefully. Your safety and the safety of others depend on it. The reading process can help.

Before Reading

Use the reading process and the strategy of skimming to help you read and respond to a state driver's handbook.

 A **Set a Purpose**

In most cases, your purpose for reading a driver's handbook will be quite clear: to prepare for the written examination to get a driver's permit.

- **To set your purpose, ask questions about the material you're about to read.**

Directions: Write three purpose questions for reading a driver's handbook. Then, make predictions about the text.

My purpose is to learn:

1.

2.

3.

My predictions:

I think the easiest parts of a driver's handbook will be

I think the most challenging parts will be

Everyday

197

B Preview

Preview to get a sense of the information you're about to read.

Directions: Preview these two pages from a driver's handbook. Make notes on the stickies.

> ◇ Driver's Handbook ◇
>
> Most traffic crashes occur at intersections or in large parking lots that are open to public use, such as at malls and grocery stores. To avoid such crashes, you must understand the right-of-way rules and how to make proper turns.
>
> ## RIGHT-OF-WAY
>
> A **traffic conflict** is a situation in which a traffic crash might occur, no matter what the traffic signs, signals, and pavement markings tell the driver. An example of a traffic conflict is a car that is making a left-hand turn at a green light and a car that wants to proceed straight through. In this case, the two cars have a traffic conflict.
>
> Our state (and all others) have a way of resolving traffic conflicts. We use what are called **right-of-way rules**. Right-of-way rules tell the drivers who gets to go first and who must wait.
>
>   ✳ ✳ ✳**Here are the right-of-way rules and examples of how they apply on the road.**
>
> ✳   *A driver approaching an intersection must yield the right-of-way to traffic already lawfully using the intersection.*
>
> **Example:** You are approaching an intersection that has a green light. Your plan is to drive straight through the intersection. Another vehicle is already in the intersection, turning left. You must let that vehicle complete its turn before you enter the intersection.
>
> ✳   *When two drivers arrive at an intersection from opposite directions at about the same time, the driver turning left must yield to approaching traffic that is going straight or turning right.*
>
> **Example:** You approach a green light with the intention of making a left-hand turn. A vehicle approaching from the opposite direction plans to go straight through the intersection. You must wait for the approaching car and any other traffic to go through the light before you can make your turn. When approaching traffic clears or stops for a red light, complete your turn.
>
> ✳   *At intersections that are not controlled by signs or signals, the driver on the left must yield the right-of-way to the driver on the right. This is also true in cases in which two vehicles arrive at a stop sign at the same time.*
>
> **Example:** You are stopped at a stop sign, and you are going to go straight through the intersection. A driver on the intersecting road has stopped at a stop sign on your right and is also going to go straight. You must yield the right-of-way to the other driver.
>
> ✳   *A vehicle entering a roadway from a driveway, alley, private road, or any other place that is*

NAME ....

Driver's Handbook

not a roadway must stop and yield the right-of-way to traffic on the roadway, as well as to pedestrians.

Example: You are driving down your driveway and have your signal on to turn left onto the street. In this case, you must yield to cars approaching from your left and from your right. If a pedestrian were crossing at the end of your driveway, you would have to wait for him or her to cross as well.

❋ *Drivers must yield to pedestrians legally using marked or unmarked crosswalks.*

Example: You are stopped at a red light. A group of adults step into the crosswalk just as the light turns green. You must yield the right-of-way to the entire group. You also must yield the right-of-way to pedestrians in crosswalks on your left or right before turning.

❋ *It is illegal to block an intersection. For this reason, you may not enter an intersection if traffic is backed up on the other side and you cannot get all the way through the intersection. You must wait until traffic ahead clears before moving into the intersection.*

Example: You are stopped at a red light. Ahead, there is a traffic jam caused by road construction. When the light turns green, you must wait until there is enough room for your vehicle to make it all the way through the intersection before you can proceed.

❋ *A driver entering a traffic circle must yield the right-of-way to drivers already in the circle.*

Example: You are stopped at a stop sign preparing to enter a traffic circle. Several cars already on the circle approach from your right. You must wait for these cars to pass and the road to be clear before you enter the circle. Keep in mind that this rule also applies to pedestrians crossing legally in marked or unmarked sidewalks.

What I learned from
the headings:
....
....
....
....

Boldface terms I
noticed:
....
....
....
....

I also noticed:
....
....
....
....

Everyday

Plan

After your preview, make a plan for reading. Choose a strategy that will help you get the information you need and remember what you've learned.

- **The reading strategy of skimming works well with most nonfiction texts, including a driver's handbook.**

During Reading

D Read with a Purpose

Remember that a large part of your purpose is to find the information you need to do well on the driver's permit exam.

Directions: Now, do a careful reading of the two sample pages from a driver's handbook. Write your Key Word or Topic Notes below.

Key Word or Topic Notes

Key Word or Topic	Notes
traffic conflict	
right-of-way rules	
example of when you yield the right-of-way	
example of when you have the right-of-way	

NAME ....

FOR USE WITH PAGES 571–580

Using the Strategy

You can use the strategy of skimming to help you prepare for the driver's exam. Reading tools, such as Study Cards and webs, will come in handy.

Directions: Make notes on these Study Cards. Then, write key details about right-of-way on the Web.

Study Cards

Right-of-way rules

Example of when the driver must yield the right-of-way

Web

"Yielding the right-of-way"

Everyday

E Connect

You'll have a better chance of remembering what you've read in a driver's handbook if you connect the information to your own life.

• Visualizing how you'll apply a rule can help you remember it.

Directions: Make a sketch that shows when you would yield the right-of-way to a car turning left. Then, make another sketch that shows when the car turning left must yield to you.

After Reading

After you finish the driver's handbook, ask yourself, "Have I accomplished what I set out to do?"

F Pause and Reflect

Ask yourself questions about the text and your purpose for reading.

• **Return to your original purpose and reflect on what you've learned.**

Directions: Answer these questions about the sample driver's handbook.

Looking Back

1. What is most important for you to remember from the right-of-way pages?

....

....

....

....

....

2. What would you like to find out more about?

....

....

....

....

....

G Reread

If you're not 100 percent sure that you've taken everything in on a first reading, you'll need to do some rereading.

• **A powerful rereading strategy to use with real-world writing is visualizing and thinking aloud.**

Directions: Write a Think Aloud in which you explain how you would make a right-hand turn from a side road into a traffic circle.

Everyday

Think Aloud

....
....
....
....
....
....
....

H Remember

Good readers remember what they've read, especially if they know they're going to be tested on the material later.

• **Asking "What if" questions can help you remember what you've read in a driver's handbook.**

Directions: Answer these "What if" questions. Then, write two of your own.

Questions

1. What if you arrive at an intersection after a car has pulled into the intersection to make a left?

....

....

2. What if you are pulling out of a parking lot at a green light, but there continues to be some

oncoming traffic?

....

3. My question:

....

....

4. My question:

....

....

Focus on Reading Instructions

Almost anything you buy will come with a set of instructions. Some are quite easy to read, but others will be more challenging. The reading process can help.

Step 1 Set your purpose.

You'll probably have a purpose in mind before you pick up the instructions. Think about this purpose as you thumb through the text and diagrams. Mark the parts that you know you need to read.

Directions: What would your purpose be for reading instructions on how to store phone numbers in your phone's memory? Write it here.

My purpose:

Step 2 Read carefully.

Next, read the instructions and make notes. Use the strategy of close reading to help you understand the most important words and phrases. Read and reread these important details until you're sure you know what they're saying.

Directions: Read the set of instructions that follows. Highlight the most important details.

from *About Your Cordless Telephone*

MEMORY DIALING: STORING NUMBERS

You can store up to 20 digits including #, *, and PAUSE as a telephone number. Follow these instructions.

Pick up your handset. Press and hold MEM till a beep sounds.

Enter a two-digit number from 01–20. This will be the memory number for the first telephone number you want to store.

Press SELECT. The LCD displays the following screen:

```
                 STORE NUMBER
3:16 PM                    4/08


NEW CALLS 2
STORED CALLS 2
```

Everyday

from *About Your Cordless Telephone*

Enter a telephone number to be stored.

Press SELECT. A confirmation beep sounds and the number is stored.

The next LCD screen will prompt you to type in a name of up to 14 characters. Use the ⇑ and ⇓ keys to choose the alphanumeric characters.

Press SELECT. A confirmation beep sounds and the name is stored.

The LCD returns to Memory Store screen. To store more numbers, return to step two. To finish the operation, press MEM or simply hang up the phone.

Step 3 Think aloud.

As you read directions, it can help to think aloud.

Directions: Write a Think Aloud that tells the steps involved in storing numbers in a cordless phone's memory. Be as detailed as possible.

Think Aloud

1.

2.

3.

4.

5.

Focus on Reading for Work

At work, you'll read a variety of texts. These will likely include employee handbooks, schedules, and memos. The reading process can help.

Step 1 Identify your purpose.

Think about what you need to know before you begin reading work-related materials.

Directions: Here, you'll read a sample of a company dress code policy. Imagine you are an employee of this company. What would be your purpose for reading the policy? Write it on the lines below.

My purpose: ....

Step 2 Understand the organization.

A quick preview of the text can help you understand how it is organized. This in turn can help you find the information you need.

Directions: Preview the sample dress code policy on page 208. Make notes on the Preview Chart below.

Preview Chart

What is the subject of the policy statement?	Who wrote it?
Understanding a Policy	
When was it written?	For whom was it written?

Everyday

Computer Solutions, Inc.

325 West 87th Street

New York, New York 10103

April 2002

From the Human Resources Department

To All Employees

Dress Code Policy

Policy:

It is the policy of Computer Solutions, Inc., that each employee's dress, grooming, and personal hygiene should be appropriate to the work situation.

Specifically:

1. Employees are expected to present at all times a professional, business-like image to customers and the public. Radical departures from conventional dress or personal grooming and hygiene standards are not permitted.

2. Office workers must comply with the following standards:

   a. Employees should dress in a manner that is normally acceptable in business establishments. Employees should not wear jeans, athletic clothing, T-shirts, shorts, sandals, novelty buttons, baseball hats, or other items that do not present a business-like appearance.

   b. Hair should be clean, combed, and neatly trimmed or arranged. Shaggy, unkempt hair is not permitted.

   c. Facial hair of any kind must be kept clean and neatly trimmed.

   d. Tattoos and body piercings (other than earrings) should not be visible.

3. Any employee who does not meet the standards of this policy will be required to take corrective action. This may include being asked to leave the premises. Employees will not be compensated for work time missed because of failure to comply with the Dress Code Policy.

This policy applies to ....

....

....

....

The numbered list ....

tells me ....

....

....

....

What is the purpose of ....

item # 3? ....

....

....

....

NAME

Step 3 Find out what you need to know.

Use the strategy of skimming to find the information you need.

Directions: Read the Dress Code Policy statement. Highlight key words and phrases. Make notes on the stickies.

Step 4 Apply the information to your own life.

Not everything you read in a workplace handbook, memo, or schedule will apply to you personally. But you need to find a way to keep track of the information that *does* apply to you. Making notes to yourself can help.

Directions: Imagine you are preparing for your first day of work at Computer Solutions, Inc. Make a few notes to yourself about the dress code policy. Write only the information that applies to you.

From the desk of

Dress Code at Computer Solutions, Inc.:

Everyday

Reading Tests

The reading process and the strategy of skimming can help you answer the questions on just about any type of test you take. Practice the steps here.

Before Reading

Preparing beforehand is key to doing well on a test. On the day of the test, you'll set your purpose and then use the strategy of skimming to help you answer the questions.

A Set a Purpose

No matter what type of test you are taking, your purpose will be to figure out what the test questions are asking and then decide what information is needed for the answers.

• **To set your purpose, ask questions about the test and test questions.**

Directions: For this sample test, you'll read a short excerpt called "An Anniversary Photograph." Write your purpose questions here.

My purpose questions: ....

....

....

....

....

....

....

....

....

B Preview

Once you've set your purpose, begin the important task of previewing. If you're permitted, glance through the entire test. Try to get a sense of what the questions are like.

Directions: Preview the sample test that follows. Make notes on the stickies.

Midterm Reading Test

30 Minutes—4 Questions, 1 Essay

DIRECTIONS: Circle the letter of the correct answer to each question. You will not be penalized for incorrect answers. Write your essay in the blue test booklet.

MIDTERM REVIEW, PASSAGE #1

from *Thirteen Senses: A Memoir* by Victor Villaseñor

"An Anniversary Photograph"

The father sun, the blanket of the poor, was going down. The whole tribe of the Villaseñors went outside to have their picture taken.

Carlota, *"Tia Tota,"* as all the children called her, moved quickly with her cane in hand and took the main chair in the middle of the picture, sitting to Salvador's right and forcing her sister Lupe to sit on Salvador's left. And so this was how Salvador and Lupe's golden anniversary picture was taken, with *Tia Tota* sitting proudly in the center with her five-foot-two frame looking so large and tall and imposing as she faced straight into the camera.

Tia Tota really thought that she was the queen of the whole show, with her large, blonde wig, white-powdered face, and a huge white flower pinned above her heart area, wanting so desperately to hide her dark Indian blood and look All-American White.

Salvador was looking off into the distance toward his right, holding his black, thick-rim glasses on his lap with both of his hands. Lupe had one grandchild and one great-grandchild on her lap. She was completely oblivious to their picture being taken—she was so happy playing with these newest additions of *la familia.*

And standing behind Salvador and Lupe were their four children, Tencha, Victor, Linda, and Teresita, and their families.

It was a telling picture.

Passage #1 Multiple-choice Questions

1. "An Anniversary Photograph" is an example of what kind of writing?

    A. expository writing   C. autobiographical writing

    B. persuasive writing   D. fictional writing

Tests

Midterm Reading Test

2. In the phrase "large and tall and imposing," the word *imposing* means
    A. unhappy   C. intimidating
    B. angry   D. greedy

3. "The father sun, the blanket of the poor" is an example of a
    A. metaphor   C. simile
    B. alliteration   D. hyperbole

4. What is the author's attitude toward Tia Tota?
    A. He adores her.   C. He fears her.
    B. He despises her.   D. He understands her.

Essay Question

5. Explain what you think the author means by "It was a telling picture." Use details from the excerpt to support what you say.

I have this much time to complete the test:

I predict the reading will be about:

I learned this from the directions:

I noticed this about the test questions:

 **Plan**

Most tests contain a combination of fact and inference questions. Choose a strategy that can help you correctly answer both types of questions.

> • **The strategy of skimming can help you find the answers you need in the shortest amount of time.**

When you skim, pay attention to:

❑ headings or headlines

❑ boldface words

❑ repeated words

❑ bulleted lists or text in italics

During Reading

D **Read with a Purpose**

A slow and careful reading of the whole passage or test item is absolutely essential.

Directions: Go back now to page 211 and read the passage entitled "An Anniversary Photograph." Underline important words or phrases. Then, summarize the passage here.

My summary: ....

....

....

....

....

....

....

....

....

Tests

Using the Strategy

Once you've read the passage, you can begin answering the questions. Read each question. Skim the passage for answers.

Directions: Read the four multiple-choice questions on pages 211–212. Highlight the key words in each. Then, tell where you should skim to find the answers.

Question #	Where I'll Begin Skimming
1	
2	
3	
4	

Understanding How Tests Are Organized

Usually, the most challenging questions will appear at the end of the test.

Directions: Reread question #4. Then, explain which words and sentences in the reading provide clues about the author's attitude.

Clues I found: ....

....

....

The author's attitude toward Tia Tota is ....

....

....

E Connect

Connecting to a test means thinking about what you've learned elsewhere and using what you recall to answer the question.

• **Connect to an essay question by recording your thoughts and feelings about the subject.**

Directions: Reread the essay question. Then, write what you know about the topic on the sticky.

Essay Question

5. Explain what you think the author means by "It was a telling picture." Use details from the excerpt to support what you say.

What I know about the phrase
"a telling picture":

....

....

....

....

After Reading

When you finish taking a test, take a moment or two to think about which parts you feel you understood easily and which parts were more difficult.

F Pause and Reflect

When you finish a test, spend a moment reviewing your work. Are there any questions that you skipped? Are there questions you'd like to return to and rethink your answer?

- **Remember your reading purpose: To find out what the test questions are asking and figure out what information is needed to answer them.**

Directions: Answer these questions about the sample test.

Pause and Reflect Questions

Which question did you think was easiest? Why?

....

....

....

Which did you find most challenging? Why?

....

....

....

Tests

NAME ....

FOR USE WITH PAGES 599–616

G Reread

At this point, return to the most challenging questions, and try visualizing and thinking aloud.

- **Visualizing and thinking aloud can help you "see" the answer to a question more clearly.**

Directions: Reread the essay question. Then, write a Think Aloud that tells how you would answer it.

‹Think Aloud›

....

....

....

....

....

....

....

H Remember

You might be tempted to stuff the test in a drawer after your teacher gives it back to you, but resist the temptation. Spend a moment reflecting on how you did. Figure out why you had trouble in certain places.

- **Note which test questions you found difficult. They might show up again on another exam.**

Directions: Exchange books with a partner and grade each other's tests. Be sure to comment on your partner's Think Aloud.

I can improve my test-taking abilities by
....

....

....

....

....

Focus on English Tests

Often in English class, you will be tested on your vocabulary and your knowledge of grammar, usage, and mechanics. Follow these steps to improve your score.

Step 1 Preview.

As a first step, try to get a sense of the types of questions you'll be expected to answer. Then, mark any key words that tell you how to answer them.

Directions: Preview the three parts of this sample test. Underline key words in each question.

◁ Sample Test ▷

Part 1 Vocabulary

1. If JECT means "to throw," what does *reject* mean?

A. throw to   B. throw again   C. throw back   D. throw under

Part 2 Grammar

2. *The young children moved quickly toward the exit ramp after their teacher said "Hurry!"*

In the above sentence, the word *quickly* functions as a(n)

A. adjective   B. conjunction   C. adverb   D. preposition

Part 3 Usage and mechanics

3. *My sister and _____ visited a museum last year.*

Choose the word that best completes the above sentence.

A. I   B. us   C. them   D. her

Step 2 Eliminate incorrect answers.

Next, eliminate the answers that you know are clearly wrong.

Directions: Return to the three questions. Cross out as many incorrect answers as you can.

Tests

Step 3 Use your strategies.

When answering vocabulary questions, use word strategies such as searching for context clues. When answering grammar and usage questions, use the reading strategy of thinking aloud.

Directions: Write Think Alouds for the three questions.

To answer question #1, I need to ....

....

To answer question #2, I need to ....

....

To answer question #3, I need to ....

....

Step 4 Figure out word relationships.

Save any word analogy questions for last. To solve them, figure out how the given word pair is related. Then find a pair that has the same relationship.

Directions: Read this analogy question. Make notes on the sticky.

odometer : distance :: _____
A. ruby : diamond   C. icing : cake
B. stopwatch : time   D. merciless : sympathetic

How odometer and distance
are related:
....

....

The correct answer is

because

....

....

Focus on Writing Tests

Here's a plan that you can use to help raise your writing test scores.

Step 1 Read carefully the directions and prompts.

Your first step on any writing test is to read carefully the directions and the writing prompts. Underline information about the type of writing you're to do and the subject you're being asked to write about.

<u>Directions:</u> Read the following essay assignment and writing prompt. Underline any key words and phrases. Then, make notes on the sticky.

Sample Test

PROMPT: Your school board is considering a proposal that would add an additional school holiday to the district calendar. You have been asked to write an essay to convince school board members to vote in favor of this new holiday. What will you say to convince them?

DIRECTIONS: Write an essay in which you persuade your school board to add a new school holiday to the district calendar. Explain what the holiday would be, and then state why it is needed. Offer at least three pieces of support for your opinion. Be sure to proofread your work when you've finished.

The subject of the essay is:

The type of essay I'm to write is:

What I need to do to write the essay:

1.

2.

3.

4.

Tests

Step 2 Write your thesis statement.

Your next step is to write a thesis statement for your essay.

Directions: Use the formula below to write an opinion statement for the school holiday essay.

subject
+
my thoughts and feelings about the subject
=
my thesis/thesis statement

....

....

....

Step 3 Organize.

Take a moment to organize your essay before you begin writing.

Directions: Use this organizer to plan your school holiday essay.

Main Idea Organizer

My opinion: Vote yes for a new school holiday, as it will benefit everyone at the school.		
Detail 1	**Detail 2**	**Detail 3**

Use a combination of personal details and details from other sources, including facts, figures, examples, and ideas from "experts."

NAME

Step 4 Write and proofread.

Put your thesis statement in the introduction. Discuss your support in the body of the essay. Finish with a restatement of your thesis or opinion.

Directions: Write a short essay on why for your school needs a new holiday. Proofread it carefully.

....

....

....

....

....

....

....

....

....

....

....

....

....

Tests

Focus on Standardized Tests

Standardized tests examine the breadth of your knowledge in key academic subjects, including math, English, science, and history. The key to doing well on these kinds of tests is staying focused and reading carefully.

Step 1 Read the directions.

You need to read the test directions carefully. If you are permitted to write in the test booklet, underline key words and phrases.

Directions: Read these sample test directions. Underline any key words.

Sample Test

DIRECTIONS: Mark only one answer to each question. You will NOT be penalized for wrong answers, so it is in your best interest to answer every question on the test, even if you must make a guess. When you've finished with a section, close your book. Do not move on to the next section of the test until you are told to do so.

Step 2 Read each question.

Read the questions one at a time. Try to think of the answers to questions *before* you look at the choices given.

Directions: Read this sample question. Make notes on the sticky.

Sample Test

You can divide Shakespeare's plays into four dramatic categories. The categories are:

The question is asking me to:

....

....

My answer:

....

....

....

Step 3 Read the answers.

Next, read every possible answer to the question, even if you're sure you know the correct one. Eliminate answers that are clearly wrong.

Directions: Read the four possible answers to the Shakespeare question. Eliminate answers that are clearly wrong. Make notes on the sticky.

> **Sample Test**
>
> A. Comedies, Histories, Love Stories, Sonnets
> B. Comedies, Tragedies, Histories, Romances
> C. Comedies, Tragedies, Farces, Romances
> D. Comedies, Tragedies, Histories, Thrillers

Step 4 Make an educated guess.

If you absolutely do not know the correct answer, make an educated guess. The strategy of thinking aloud can help.

Directions: Write a Think Aloud in which you explain the correct answer to the Shakespeare question. Explain how you arrived at the answer.

> **Think Aloud**

_____

_____

_____

_____

_____

_____

_____

_____

Tests

Focus on History Tests

Most history tests examine your ability to read critically, recall key facts, and interpret graphics. Following this four-step plan can help.

Step 1 Read each question.

Answer the easiest questions first, but be sure to read each question carefully, no matter how easy it seems.

Directions: Read this sample question.

> **Sample Question**
>
> 1. Which of these is NOT a reason for the fall of Rome?
>   A. Most Roman citizens were heavily taxed.
>   B. Small farmers could not compete with large landowners.
>   C. Diseases killed about one-third of the population.
>   D. The plebeians staged a revolution against the patricians.

To answer this question, I need to _____

Step 2 Rule out wrong answers.

Next, read every answer choice, even if you know the correct one. Eliminate incorrect answers as you go.

Directions: Return to the sample question. Cross out answers that are clearly wrong. Then, answer the sample test question on the lines below.

My answer is _____ because _____

Step 3 With graphics, look at the big picture.

You may want to leave the graphics questions for last, since these are often the most challenging. With each new graphic, ask yourself, "What can this graphic tell me?"

Directions: Study this graphic. Then read the question. Make notes on the sticky.

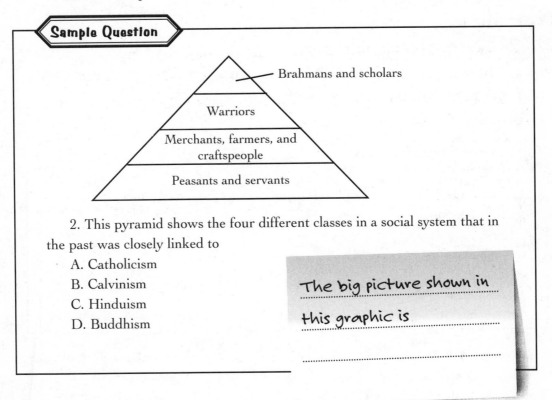

Sample Question

Brahmans and scholars

Warriors

Merchants, farmers, and craftspeople

Peasants and servants

2. This pyramid shows the four different classes in a social system that in the past was closely linked to

    A. Catholicism
    B. Calvinism
    C. Hinduism
    D. Buddhism

The big picture shown in this graphic is

Step 4 Talk through the answers.

Then use the strategy of thinking aloud to help you sort through the answers to the question.

Directions: Take another look at the graphic, and reread the question. Eliminate answers that are clearly wrong. Then, write a Think Aloud that explains the correct answer and how you arrived at it.

Think Aloud

....
....
....
....

Tests

Focus on Math Tests

You can do well on a math test even if math is not your best subject. The trick is to read each question slowly and carefully.

Step 1 Preview.

As always, preview the test before you begin writing. Mark the easiest questions with an asterisk. Mark the key words in the questions as you go.

Directions: Preview the sample test. Underline any key words in each question.

> ### Sample Test
>
> 1. A child's pool holds 45 liters of water and it fills at a rate of 3.3 liters per minute. How long, to the nearest minute, will it take to fill the pool?
>   A. 12 minutes
>   B. 14 minutes
>   C. 15 minutes
>   D. 17 minutes
>
> 2. Last week at Millbrook School, 6 students were absent on Monday, 4 students were absent on Tuesday, 3 students were absent on Wednesday, and 7 students were absent on both Thursday and Friday. What was the average daily absentee rate at Millbrook for this week?
>   A. 9 students
>   B. 7 students
>   C. 5 students
>   D. 3 students

Step 2 Eliminate.

Next, read each question and its answer choices. Eliminate those that are clearly wrong.

Directions: Return to the sample test. Cross out the answers you know are wrong.

Step 3 Estimate.

If possible, try to estimate the answer. Check to see if there is an answer that is close to your estimate.

Directions: Look at question 1 again. Then estimate how many minutes it will take to fill the pool.

I estimate that it will take ____ minutes, so the answer to question 1 is ____

Step 4 Visualize.

If you get stuck, try to visualize what the problem is saying.

Directions: Make a sketch that reflects question 2. Then solve the problem.

....
....
....
....
....
....
....

Step 5 Check.

As a final step, check your work. Use a different method to solve the same problem.

Directions: In column 1 is an equation you can use to solve question 1. Write a different way to solve the same question in column 2.

Equation 1	Equation 2
$45 \div 3.3 = n$	

Focus on Science Tests

To do well on a science test, you must be able to recall important concepts and use reasoning skills. The reading process can help. Follow these steps.

Step 1 Read.

As a first step, preview the test. Then, read the individual questions and any graphics.

Directions: Read the table. Think about the big picture. Then read the question and make notes on the stickies.

The Five Brightest Stars

Star Apparent Magnitude

	Brightness Factor	Distance from Earth in Light Years
Arcturus	–0.06	36
Canopus	–0.73	650
Centauri	–0.01	4
Rigel	–0.14	540

*The smaller the brightness number, the brighter the star.

1. What can you conclude about the relationship between the apparent magnitude of a star and its distance from Earth?

....

2. Which of these statements cannot be supported with facts from the chart?
   A. Arcturus is closer to Earth than Canopus.
   B. Rigel is farther from Earth than Centauri.
   C. Rigel is farther from Earth than Canopus.
   D. Of the four stars, Centauri is closest to Earth.

The graphic shows
....
....
....

I notice that
....
....
....

Step 2 Read the questions.

Next, read the questions. See if you know each answer without looking at the choices.

Directions: Read the two questions on the sample test. Underline key words. Then, make notes on the lines below.

To answer this question, I need to

To answer this question, I need to

Step 3 Use the strategy of thinking aloud.

Any time you're stumped by a question, use the strategy of thinking aloud. It will help you talk your way through to the correct answer.

Directions: Complete this Think Aloud for the two questions on the sample test.

◄ Think Aloud

For Question 1:

For Question 2:

Tests

NAME ....

FOR USE WITH PAGES 659–666

Learning New Words

Good readers know that mastering new words is important.
Focusing on unfamiliar words one by one will help you build
a better vocabulary. These tips can help.

Step 1 Read.

Watch for unfamiliar words as you read.

Directions: Read this paragraph from an essay about Ernest Hemingway.
Circle any unfamiliar words.

from "Hemingway: The Old Lion" by Malcolm Cowley

When Hemingway came back from the wars for the last time, in March 1945, he
was the most famous writer in the world and he had chosen—or the public had chosen
for him—the most obdurate problem he could bring himself to face. He must, the
public said—and his friends took for granted, and Hemingway himself seems to have
felt—he must write a novel about World War II that would be bigger in every way
than his novel about the Spanish Civil War. For this he had more than enough
material, all gathered at first hand, but there were obstacles to the writing of which the
public and even his friends had no conception.

Step 2 Record.

Keep track of unfamiliar words by writing them in a vocabulary journal.

Directions: Record unfamiliar words from the paragraph in the journal on
the next page. Also, write down the sentences or phrases in which you
found the words.

NAME

FOR USE WITH PAGES 659–666

Vocabulary Journal

	English
	from "Hemingway: The Old Lion," p. 225
	Unfamiliar words
●	1.
	Definition:
	2.
	Definition:
	3.
	Definition:

Step 3 Define.

Use context clues, word parts, or a dictionary to define each word. For information on these strategies, see pages 666–681 in the *Reader's Handbook*.

Directions: Go back to the vocabulary journal and add definitions for the unfamiliar words from the Cowley paragraph.

Step 4 Use.

The best way to remember a word you've collected is to use it in conversation or in your writing.

Directions: Write one sentence for each of the words you defined.

My Sentences

Vocabulary

Skills for Learning New Words

There are other ways to figure out the meaning of a word besides checking a dictionary. These include using context clues and word parts.

Step 1 Use context clues.

When you come to an unfamiliar word, try defining it by its context. This means checking the text that surrounds the word to see if you can find clues about the unfamiliar word's meaning.

Directions: Read this paragraph from Edgar Allan Poe's short story "The Fall of the House of Usher." Use context clues to figure out the meaning of the underlined words.

from "The Fall of the House of Usher" by Edgar Allan Poe

The disease of the lady Madeline had long baffled the skill of her physicians. A settled apathy, a gradual wasting away of the person, and frequent although transient affections of a partially cataleptical character were the unusual diagnosis. Hitherto she had steadily born up against the pressure of her <u>malady</u>, and had not betaken herself finally to bed; but on the closing in of the evening of my arrival at the house, she <u>succumbed</u> (as her brother told me at night with inexpressible agitation) to the <u>prostrating</u> power of the destroyer; and I learned that the glimpse I had obtained of her person would thus probably be the last I should obtain—that the lady, at least while living, would be seen by me no more.

Underlined Words	My Definition	Context Clues I Used
malady		
succumbed		
prostrating		

NAME ....

Step 2 Use word parts.

If you can't find context clues, check to see if there are any familiar word parts—root words, prefixes, or suffixes.

Directions: Reread the final sentence of the Poe paragraph. Then complete this word tree by adding words that have the root *tain*. Use what you've learned to define the words you've written in the tree.

Root Words

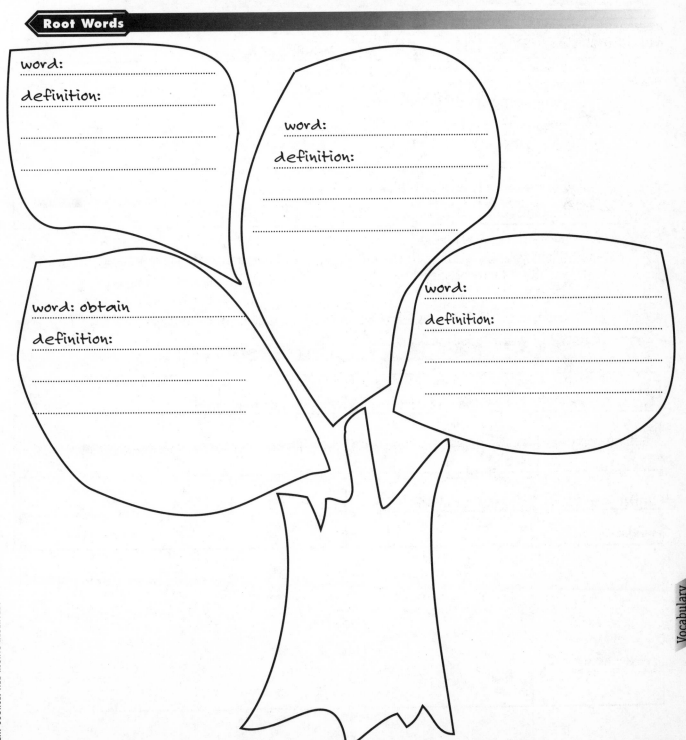

word:

definition:

word:

definition:

word: obtain

definition:

word:

definition:

Vocabulary

If you know the meaning of the prefix, you have a clue about the meaning of the whole word.

Directions: Add a prefix to each of the words on the list. Then, tell what the new word means.

anti-, ant- = against   *ir-* = not   *mis-* = incorrect, bad

Prefixes

Prefix + Word	New Word	Meaning of New Word
1. + *regular*		
2. + *acid*		
3. + *replaceable*		
4. + *social*		
5. + *take*		

When you add a suffix to the end of a word, you change its meaning and usually its part of speech. Suffixes can also give you clues about an unfamiliar word's meaning.

-ology = study of *-ance* = action, state of, quality of *-ful* = full of

Suffixes

Word+ Suffix	New Word	Meaning of New Word
1. bio +		
2. vigil +		
3. fright +		
4. confer +		

Dictionary  Dipping

Good readers have a dictionary at their side when they read. They are prepared to look up unfamiliar words. Without even realizing it, they follow these two steps when searching for the definition of a word.

Step 1 Read.

If you come to an unfamiliar word and can't define it on your own, use a dictionary. First, find the entry. Then read it carefully.

Directions: Read this sample entry. Then answer the questions.

> **Dictionary Entry**
>
> **inarticulate** (in' är tic' u lit) *adj.* not uttered in distinct syllables or words: *an inarticulate mutter.* 2. unable to speak in words; dumb: *inarticulate with grief.* 3. not able to put one's thoughts and feelings into words easily and clearly. —**inarticulately** *adv.* —**inarticulateness** *n.*

What part of speech is *inarticulate?*

....

What is the adverbial form of *inarticulate?*

....

Which syllables are stressed in *inarticulate?*

....

How many definitions does the word *inarticulate* have?

....

Step 2 Remember.

The easiest way to remember a new word is to use it again and again.

Directions: Write a sentence using *inarticulate* and another using *inarticulately.*

Sentence #1 ....

....

Sentence #2 ....

....

Vocabulary

Focus on Using a Thesaurus

A thesaurus is a large list of synonyms. It is a tool you can use to expand your vocabulary.

Step 1 Read.

Your thesaurus can help you find synonyms for a given word. First, find the entry for the word in question. Then, read the entire entry carefully (antonyms are listed after the dash).

Directions: Read this entry for *futile*. Then answer the questions.

> **Thesaurus Entry**
>
> **futile,** *adj.* vain, useless, in vain, fruitless, hopeless, impractical, worthless, unprofitable, to no effect, not successful, to no purpose, unneeded, unsatisfactory, unsatisfying, ineffective, ineffectual, unproductive, idle, empty, hollow, unreal—hopeful, practical, effective.

1. What part of speech is futile?

....

....

2. What are some synonyms for *futile?*

....

....

3. What are some antonyms?

....

....

Step 2 Remember.

Using the synonyms you find can help you remember.

Directions: Use synonyms for *futile* to complete these sentences. Then use synonyms in five sentences of your own.

1. That is a _____ idea.

2. She worked ....

3. The situation was absolutely ....

4. She shut off the main valve ....

5. They went on a _____ search for the missing wallet.

My Sentences:

1. ....

....

....

2. ....

....

....

3. ....

....

....

4. ....

....

....

5. ....

....

....

Vocabulary

Analogies

To complete an analogy, find a pair of words that explore the same relationship as the given set of words.

Step 1 Analyze the original pair.

As a first step, read the analogy carefully. Figure out the relationship between the given pair of words.

Directions: Read the sample analogies. Make notes on the stickies.

Sample Analogies

1. bagel : bread :: rat :
A. mouse
B. rodent
C. trap
D. exterminator

2. rage : anger :: sadness :
A. fury
B. crying
C. complaining
D. misery

How bagel and bread are related:

How rage and anger are related:

Step 2 Explore possible answers.

First eliminate any answers that are clearly wrong. Then, explore the word pairs that remain. The strategy of thinking aloud can help.

Directions: Return to the sample analogies. Cross out any answers that are clearly wrong. Then, write Think Alouds to show how you decided on the correct answer.

Think Aloud

To answer Analogy 1, I need to

To answer Analogy 2, I need to

....

....

....

....

....

Step 3 Study.

It's a good idea to learn the most common types of relationships explored in analogies.

Directions: Reread pages 687–689 in the *Reader's Handbook*. Then, write an example for each type of analogy listed below. Write examples that are different from the ones in the *Handbook*.

◄ **Relationships in Analogies**

1. Antonym

flippant : deferential :: ....

2. Part of a Whole (Is a Part of)

star : constellation :: ....

3. Item and What It Is Designed to Do (Is Used to)

scale : weight :: ....

4. Action and Where It Takes Place (Is a Place Where)

aquarium : fish :: ....

5. Result and Who Does It (Is Done by)

web : spider :: ....

6. Class and Example of That Class (Class and Subclass)

flower : tulip :: ....

7. Name and a Word That Describes It

chips : crisp :: ....

8. Sequence

bulb : tulip :: ....

Vocabulary

Author/Title Index

Photo Credits

23 © Photodisc

33 © The Natural History Museum, London

34 © Russ Finley Photography

35 © José Manuel Sanchis Calvete/ Corbis

86 © Bettman/Corbis

95 Courtesy Library of Congress

184 © Photodisc